Simple and on point. The relevance of local churches in the West rests on these principles.

DAVE RUNYON
Coauthor of *The Art of Neighboring* and director of CityUnite

Jesus' response to a question about which neighbors are worthy of our love is to say, in effect, "Just be a neighbor." In *Staying Is the New Going*, Alan Briggs offers us a winsome and practical exploration of an oft-neglected, yet vital component of neighborliness—longevity in place. With insight garnered from experience and listening to others, *Staying Is the New Going* is a welcome addition.

SEAN GLADDING
Author of *The Story of God, the Story of Us* and *TEN: Words of Life for an Addicted, Compulsive, Cynical, Divided and Worn-out Culture*

Jesus plants his people—the people of the Kingdom—in a context. This includes family, workplace, culture, and the places we live. In order to bear fruit in that place, his people must take root. In this wonderful book, we follow Alan as he sets aside wings and learns to put down roots. This book is for learners and is clearly written by a learner. It is challenging, not because the concepts are hard to understand, but because we've somehow drifted far from the timeless truths Jesus told about love for one's neighbor. I long to see God's people rooted both in Christ and in their neighborhoods. In Alan I sense a like-hearted traveler who helps me see that my greatest journey may simply be a walk around the block.

AL ENGLER
Mission director of Nav Neighbors, The Navigators

Do you have the courage to join in how God is working right around you, in your everyday life? Perhaps more importantly, do we as the church? This timely and energizing new book by Alan Briggs dares you to join a movement that's probably much closer than you imagined.

TIM SOERENS
Cofounding director of Parish Collective and coauthor of *The New Parish*

STAYING IS THE NEW GOING

STAYING
IS THE NEW
GOING

CHOOSING TO LOVE WHERE GOD PLACES YOU

ALAN BRIGGS

NAVPRESS

A NavPress resource published in alliance
with Tyndale House Publishers, Inc.

NAVPRESS⬤.

NavPress is the publishing ministry of The Navigators, an international Christian organization and leader in personal spiritual development. NavPress is committed to helping people grow spiritually and enjoy lives of meaning and hope through personal and group resources that are biblically rooted, culturally relevant, and highly practical.

For more information, visit www.NavPress.com.

Staying Is the New Going: Choosing to Love Where God Places You

Copyright © 2015 by Alan Briggs. All rights reserved.

A NavPress resource published in alliance with Tyndale House Publishers, Inc.

NAVPRESS and the NAVPRESS logo are registered trademarks of NavPress, The Navigators, Colorado Springs, CO. *TYNDALE* is a registered trademark of Tyndale House Publishers, Inc. Absence of ® in connection with marks of NavPress or other parties does not indicate an absence of registration of those marks.

The Team: Don Pape, Publisher; David Zimmerman, Acquisitions Editor
Cover design by Mark Anthony Lane II
Cover photograph of clouds copyright © Kevin Russ/Stocksy.com. All rights reserved.
Cover photograph of houses copyright © Lior Zilberstein/Stocksy.com. All rights reserved.
Cover illustration of sunburst copyright © ThunderPixels/Creative Market. All rights reserved.

Some of the anecdotal illustrations in this book are true to life and are included with the permission of the persons involved. All other illustrations are composites of real situations, and any resemblance to people living or dead is coincidental.

Library of Congress Cataloging-in-Publication Data
Briggs, Alan.
  Staying is the new going : choosing to love where God places you / Alan Briggs.
    pages cm
  Includes bibliographical references.
  ISBN 978-1-63146-479-9
  1. Witness bearing (Christianity) I. Title.
  BV4520.B647 2015
  248.5—dc23   2015021903

Printed in the United States of America

21	20	19	18	17	16	15
7	6	5	4	3	2	1

For Julie—

the wildest adventures of my life have come
through staying by your side.

Contents

Foreword

THERE WAS A TIME when American readers seemed enamored of novelists for whom the world was their oyster—writers who traveled widely, who crossed frontiers and opened their eyes to worlds readers had never dreamed of. They couldn't get enough of the novels of Jack London or Ernest Hemingway. They thrilled to the exotic stories of Joseph Conrad and James A. Michener. These writers and many like them created the myth that we must leave home and travel far and wide to experience the world and to find our life's work. They infected their readers with wanderlust. They invite us to disregard the mundane and to see home as a launching pad, never a destination.

But we oughtn't forget the marvelous American literary tradition of the distinctly provincial writer. These novelists and poets wrote out of their deep and abiding connection to their place. Many of them never left their home. All of them were profoundly shaped by the topography of their locale, its seasons, its residents, and its sense of place. It's the kind of regional writing you encounter in Thoreau and Emerson and Twain (although he also traveled widely).

You can start to understand the richness of provincial writing when you read the gorgeous poetry of Emily Dickinson and realize that there could have been no Emily Dickinson without the town of Amherst, Massachusetts. Indeed, Dickinson spent most of the last decade of her life confined to her Amherst house, producing exquisite work that wouldn't be read until after her death.

Likewise, the modernist poet William Carlos Williams was born and raised in Rutherford, New Jersey, in the same house he would move his wife into and in which he would raise his own family. It was from this house he practiced as a local doctor, making house calls to the good folk of Rutherford. It was in this very same house that he spent forty years of his spare time writing the beautifully accessible poems that would later inspire Allen Ginsberg and the Beat poets in the 1950s and '60s.

For Flannery O'Connor it was the small town of Milledgeville, Georgia. For Walker Percy, Covington, Louisiana. And would the poems of Robert Frost be the same without the shaping influence that rural New Hampshire had on him?

In this same vein, contemporary poet Wendell Berry, a native resident and farmer of Henry County, Kentucky, says, "What I stand for is what I stand on." That's something Hemingway could never have said.

Why am I telling you about America's famous provincialist writers? Because it seems to me that when it comes to Christian writing we can be enamored of the missionary adventure literature of David Livingstone or Hudson Taylor or Jim Eliot *at the expense of* those voices whose work is shaped by their devotion to land, home, place, neighborhood. I'm not telling you not to read Hudson Taylor or Ernest Hemingway. I'm not dissuading you from engaging with the ideas of nomadic church-planting consultants. Nor am I suggesting you not listen to the latest *robcast* from the latest cyber-dwelling Rob Bell. However, I am asking you not to engage these translocal voices *at the expense of* the provincial, the local, or the regional. We need to hear the voices of those Christians who have resolved to stay—truly stay—in the places God has planted them. We need Christian versions of Dickinson, O'Connor, Percy, and Berry—which is kind of funny, because all of them were/are deeply committed Christians.

This brings me to *Staying Is the New Going* by Alan Briggs. Acknowledging that the prevailing contemporary ideal has become to "go forth"—to pursue adventure, conquest, and exploration—Alan employs the term "staying forth" to describe the intentional loyalty to place that characterizes truly incarnational expressions of godly mission. He argues passionately for distinctly *placed* forms of ministry, for unique and indigenous forms of Christ-following that grow out of the very soil in which they're planted. And in so doing he tries to countermand all the antsy Hemingway-esque energy that makes you fidgety and tells you there's a better opportunity somewhere else. That's the jittery energy our contemporary culture promotes. It lives elsewhere. It dreams only of tomorrow. It knows only the current. It's exhausting and fretful and highly agitated.

I don't hear Alan dismissing the importance of following God's call to cross the oceans, to be transplanted in new soil, to make a home in a new locale. What I hear him saying is that wherever God sends us, whether to our own hometown or across the globe, we must learn to do what William Carlos Williams did in Rutherford, New Jersey, and what Wendell Berry says he does in rural Kentucky: "Love your neighbors—not the neighbors you pick out but the ones you have." We need to settle. We need to stay. We need to learn to love, long and loyally. We need to allow our roots to drive down deeply into the soil beneath our feet.

You might be a Jack London or Ernest Hemingway, but pray that you're not. Pray that you can learn the beauty and simplicity and inherent truthfulness of staying forth. Pray that your ministry would be as sublime and as masterful as a Flannery O'Connor short story or an Emily Dickinson poem, shaped by the place from which it emerged.

Read the book you hold in your hands right now. It might change everything by calling you not to change a thing.

Michael Frost
Morling College, Sydney

Introduction

IT WAS A BEAUTIFUL spring afternoon, and I was taking the short walk to pick up my kids from school. Parents who walk the same route every day to scoop up their kids walked hurriedly by me with their heads down. No hello, not even the customary head nod, just the classic American silent treatment.

Our family was in the throes of grief and loss from the sudden and tragic loss of my mother-in-law. My wife's closest mentor, a grandma, an anchor in our community, and the best mother-in-law a guy could imagine had been ripped away from us during the joy and frenzy of Thanksgiving. I recognized in my neighbors that day the same pain we were feeling. I saw parents and neighbors who were broken and hurting, isolated, never navigating past the surface with the people around them. They were physically present but emotionally distant. They were half-decent players in the pretending game.

The neighborhood itself reflected this emotional distance.

Front porches were empty; garages were closed. Something was strangely wrong about the whole thing—but also strangely normal. Our neighborhood was lacking neighborliness. Someone needed to introduce connection into the equation.

That day God gave me missionary lenses, and I started to see the cracks: cracks in my neighborhood, cracks in my current relationships, even cracks in my city.

If you've ever seen an optometrist, you know adjusting to clear vision isn't an easy task. Seeing things you've not seen before, seeing a little too clearly, can give you a headache. I started to imagine how our neighbors longed to see these cracks filled. As I combed Scripture the next few weeks, I was reminded that the gospel can fill all of the cracks in my neighborhood. The broken people in our neighborhood weren't waiting for a government program; they were waiting for relationships. These hurting people, so uncomfortably close to us, weren't looking for handouts; they were looking for hope. We realized it was no accident God had placed us in our home. He had planted us there—not as tenants, but as missionaries.

Now, all I had to do was actually do something.

I don't mean to brag, but as a pastor and a neighbor I am extremely gifted at finding excuses. I pulled out all the best ones:

- "We won't live in this house very long."
- "They won't live here very long."

- "They'll think we're weird."
- "We have nothing in common."
- "I don't have time to add one more thing."
- "They don't have time to hang with us."
- "I will scare them off when I talk about Jesus."
- And my favorite: "Everyone in the world is my neighbor. Why should I focus on my *actual* neighbor?"

I couldn't possibly spend the precious effort to love those right in front of my face.

Perhaps you're a master of these excuses too. Where do they come from? My excuses were motivated by three things: fear of failure, a life that was far too busy, and a consumeristic view of the place I occupied.

We began to offer our lives to our neighbors, beyond the incidental encounters while taking out the trash can or picking up our kids from school. Today our parties are different. Our days off are different. Those we call friends are different. How we measure ministry is different. Our lives are different. Our family is different.

The journey into the heart of our neighborhood has been both exhilarating and routine. Both of those have been gifts from God. My fears of failure tug at me less now than they did at the beginning. My aversion to "wasting time in the neighborhood" still rears its ugly head sometimes, but more often I see my neighborhood as a valuable space.

I have led a lot of mission trips, planned a lot of events, and led a lot of ministries, but I have never experienced anything like this—what's often called "incarnational living." It's even different from starting and leading a "missional" community. I have had many chances to involve my kids in sharing our lives and our stuff with others. I have never experienced this many "holy interruptions" that yielded spiritual fruit. Prior to this paradigm shift, my heart had never truly broken for people—my neighbors and my longtime friends alike—who did not know Jesus. Previously I grabbed ministry opportunities, but now I can truly say ministry opportunities are grabbing me. More important, Jesus has gently grabbed me in a way I have never experienced.

Since God opened my eyes to my neighborhood, my family has walked with our neighbors through death and depression, shed tears and belly-laughed with school parents, and become friends with those we have next to nothing in common with. We have given gifts and received them. We have celebrated birthdays and enjoyed neighborhood game nights. For the first time I am not drawn to living in another city, moving to another neighborhood across our city, or drifting away from those I am in relationship with. For the first time my wife and I can say, "We want to stay!"

I wish it hadn't taken this long for our home to become a hub *for* ministry instead of a refuge *from* ministry. It's been a spiritual road trip, and we didn't arrive here suddenly. We've put the gospel to a test I've always wanted to take: *If we live our lives for Jesus—simply, right where we are—will we taste salty and give off a glow?* Growing roots has been, in some ways, a massive risk, but this is a vision I can't walk away from. I am voluntarily stuck. I want to refine the art of staying, of "dwelling well," as my family gives glimpses of Jesus to a city, a neighborhood, and a gaggle of friends who want hope running through their veins again.

THE NEXT FRONTIER

People everywhere are feeling this gravitational staying force. People seeking to live a Jesus life and those who don't know him alike are feeling the tug to put down roots in places and spaces again. I happen to think Christians need to hear this message the most, however, because cities are quickly becoming the lifeblood of mission. Our current places are becoming the next frontier, and neighborhoods are becoming parishes again, where churches anchor their communities and every Christian can live out our first vocation as a follower of Jesus eyeball to eyeball.

This is a return to something people understood before the global and digital age distracted us. Something in all of us wants to be connected to a place and the people who live in it. Those in our neighborhood and city are longing for it. Those I have long conversations with in the café spend much of their week chasing it. Those fully entrenched in civic clubs have invested in it. There's a collision of something beautiful happening in our world that we, as followers of Jesus, cannot afford to miss.

I write this book from the posture of a learner and a

storyteller, not an expert. If I had written a book on fleshing out Jesus in place and space five years ago, it would have had the tone of a failing cynic. In North America, ministry that could be called incarnational seems countercultural (or at least optional). Other cultures are far more communal, far more rooted. A friend of mine, who grew up as a child of missionaries in Russia, taught me a word that has shaped his view of communities and ministry: *sotrudnichestvo*, which translates roughly to "Let us do work together in our space." We have no such word in English, but what if we did? What if we invited people regularly to work for the good of our places? What if the church was again known for being the people who loved their cities and the people in them the most?

God has taken our family on a surprising and exciting journey. We have gotten serious about loving our neighbors—our literal neighbors. We've gotten serious about loving our city, a place I had previously looked for opportunities to escape. We've gotten serious about loving friends who orbit around our lives, friends whom I had once been content to abandon. This book is a call to come back home, a call to recover from farsightedness of heart. It's time for the people of Jesus to live for Jesus right where we are.

I believe in being straightforward, so here are my intentions:

I want you to examine your life and make changes that render you more local and relationally accessible.

I want you to grow spiritual roots in your current realities instead of living under a fantasy of wings.

I want you to follow Jesus into the mundane, ordinary, everyday moments of life and relationships.

I want to challenge "the success of flight" and share how people are instead choosing the faithfulness of being fully present.

I want to challenge you to rethink the exclusivity of pilgrimage. We love escaping the daily grind and retreating to euphoric and beautiful places. We seem to find God there in the mystery, but we must not find him *only* there. In his striking memoir, Eugene Peterson describes his family's annual Montana trip and the beauty and respite they experienced. One particular year the trip sparked questions in him: "Why wait for August, why wait for Montana? What's wrong with September through July, what's wrong with Maryland?"[1] I want us to ask similar questions: *What's wrong with right now in the guts of life? What's wrong with the ground you are walking on? What's wrong with the people you are already around?*

This book might frustrate you. It may bore you. It may even fall short of giving you a grand plan for changing your community and the world. I'm okay with that. I believe God is drawing his church back to ordinary, local relationships among real neighbors, whole persons in a real context, not just far-off missionary conquests. This is not a book about devoting your conquest to God; this is a book about devoting your context to him.

1

THE RESURRECTION OF PLACE

"The same restlessness that sends us searching for community also keeps us from settling down wherever we are."
JONATHAN WILSON-HARTGROVE, *THE WISDOM OF STABILITY*

A year from now we'll all be gone
All our friends will move away
And they're going to better places
THE HEAD AND THE HEART, "RIVERS AND ROADS"

SOMEHOW I THOUGHT possessing a Colorado driver's license would quench all my desires for adventure. Colorado has some of the best mountains, streams, adventure spots, and mountain towns one state could offer. But after exploring some of the mountain towns, bagging several peaks, and catching more than a few trout, I still wasn't content. So I began to scratch out a bucket list. My top three spots were Antarctica, New Zealand, and Kauai.

By a twist of fate I was offered a job working a "summer" in Antarctica. It was the coldest summer of my life. I worked long hours with the other crazies, people just like me who dreamed of traveling around the world. Some had been to every continent. Their exotic stories over hot cider in the evenings only compounded my desire to travel.

After my work season was finished I planned two adventure-packed trips, first to New Zealand and then to Kauai, exploring the mountains and coasts and surfing the breaks. Those few months were beyond my wildest dreams. I seemed to catch all the breaks in New Zealand, including the only weather window of the season to traverse ice fields and climb a world-class peak. I camped on glaciers, climbed sheer walls, kayaked past seals in crystal-clear water, stayed up late talking to other travelers in hostels, hitchhiked with generous people, watched rugby with the locals, and backpacked sites that looked more pristine than a scene from *The Lord of the Rings*. It was absolutely epic.

But just a few weeks before leaving New Zealand, I had experienced enough. I came. I saw. I took pictures. And I was done. I was feeling discontent and disconnected. I longed for something I had never longed for: home.

Then again, I had no idea where home was. My family no longer lived where I had grown up. My stuff was stored in Colorado, and I had quickly made a large pool of relational connections and developed a handful of close friendships there. But I was not invested there.

There I was, on one of the most beautiful spots on the globe, longing to belong to some place, any place, even a very ordinary place. It's as if God had given me exactly what I wanted, and I had gotten to the end of my adventure dreams. It was time to ask, "What's next?" I was even asking, "Where's next?" I was craving a basic human need, the answer to which the God of relationship has sown deep into the threads of the human soul: I needed to find rich soil and put down some roots.

Many of us are in serious need of roots. Maybe you've been in your city for years, but you've never made it your home. Maybe you are currently scheming your escape plan. I hope you will stop for long enough to consider what the impact would be if you decided to take a risk and stay. In our upwardly mobile and frenetically busy society, the joy of flight has rarely been challenged. The assumption that life is inherently better somewhere else has rarely been challenged. I think it's time we take a hard look at how our rootlessness has affected our lives and the lives around us. As followers of Jesus, what influence do we miss as our minds, hearts, and bodies whiz by on our way to other places?

ROCKS WITH NO MOSS

I remember exactly where I was sitting. I had come for a pick-me-up, not a smack in the face. "No one is more transient than American pastors, like rocks with no moss." The room was still. We all knew it was true. Michael Frost wasn't just an Aussie speaking to Americans that day; he was a prophet confronting the church.

If we were looking for the means to destroy the impact of the local church, I believe we'd place transience and disconnection high on the list. They're not spectacular, washing away our influence like a flood of scandal. They're more like a steady erosion: the church's disconnection from our communities, both in our readiness as individuals to leave one context for another and by our corporate withdrawal from direct engagement of our community, has stifled our influence and limited our capacity for relational evangelism, leaving our churches with little to no reputation in our communities, settling for occupancy.

This is a departure from the parish mentality of the past, where the church took responsibility for its context, and the people inhabiting its place. Futurist Alvin Toffler writes:

> Never in history has distance meant less. . . .
> Figuratively we "use up" places and dispose of
> them much in the same way we dispose of Kleenex
> or beer cans. We are witnessing a historic decline
> in the significance of place to human life. We are
> breeding a new race of nomads, and few suspect
> quite how massive, widespread and significant their
> migrations are.[1]

We need to ponder what message we send when we migrate—either physically, when we exit neighborhoods and cities, or emotionally, when we disengage from the real issues unfolding around us. If we never see the real issues around us, we will never see real Kingdom opportunities either. We must "dwell well" as God's people, something that "may very well be," according to the authors of *The New Parish*, "the leadership challenge of the twenty-first century."[2]

BECOMING LOCALS

"I got here as fast as I could." This is my answer when people ask if I'm a Colorado native. This is a state where being born here gives you bragging rights. Drive around and you'll see bumper stickers laying claim to the label. Even the term *native* doesn't take into account the people who were truly native to this ground, long before the railroad put this city on the map.

I originally moved to Colorado for a "work vacation." (I didn't call it "seasonal work," but I had no long-term plans to stay.) I moved here to consume what the mountains offered me. I wanted connection without commitment, like an emotional fling. Ten years after moving to this city, I can honestly say that, God willing, I'm staying. I can't slap the "Native" bumper sticker on my car, but I've become a local. You can't control whether you're a native, but you can control whether you're a local.

Locals are known. Locals are committed. Locals have found home. You find locals at cafés, at their kids' elementary school, in civic organizations, in neighborhoods—all over the place, actually. A few weeks back I was drinking a good cup of fresh roasted coffee at a local café, waiting for a friend to arrive. I watched the folks at the bar, who obviously frequent the place. They were sharing about a friend having health problems, passing around a card for him. They were organizing meals and getting the word out to visit him. The folks who frequent that café have developed into a caring community. They're locals.

Perhaps our churches need to take a lesson from the locals.

You might be tempted to upgrade to a better place, to trade in your friends, to move as far away from family dysfunction as possible. You might dream of a sexy place somewhere, where your problems are gone and people are impressed by your stories. Those are common thoughts. They just aren't realistic.

For a long time now mission has been framed as a far-off endeavor, a trip requiring a passport, a plane ticket, and a lot of packing. But God's mission is active everywhere, which means God's mission is active among your family, friends, and community. For God's work to become tangible, it must first become local, invading our everyday thinking and the places we inhabit. The ideas and dreams you have are good; they just need to be connected to actual living, breathing people with souls. This is why we pray, "Your kingdom come, your will be done, on earth [read: in this place] as it is in heaven."

God's mission of drawing wanderers into his family always takes place in the midst of ordinary places and relationships. This can take just as much energy, finances, and careful planning as a trip across the ocean. In some ways it might be more uncomfortable than sleeping on a dirt floor and eating strange food. Our mission trip started the day we were born; it ends when God calls us home. Our mission with God plays out in how we walk, talk, eat, commute, party, pray, participate, communicate, spend money, make money, and invest our time wherever we are.

This localized understanding of our God-given mission is often referred to as "faithful presence."

FAITHFUL PRESENCE

There are three key aspects to a life of faithful presence.

Incarnation. Jesus' ministry plan was to move "into the neighborhood" (John 1:14, MSG), to move from being "above" us to being "among" us. Jesus became a local among humanity; he locked into people's lives, stories, and fears when he ministered to them. He was completely present, walking, conversing, and performing life's most basic tasks with others. As Jesus exited the scene, God sent the Holy Spirit to live within his church. Our ministry plan, consequently, emulates God's. Incarnational ministry moves us from "above" our places (where we have no meaningful connection) to "among" the people, within the community.

Presence is not just physical; it's also emotional and spiritual. It has never been easier to be among people physically while remaining disconnected from them, reading e-mails on our phones or entertaining ourselves on a tablet. Living incarnational lives requires us not just to stay physically but to remain patiently, locally, and personally engaged in the spaces, opportunities, and lives around us.

Longevity. Faithfulness involves sticking something out. People are wary of "supernova ministry" that burns bright and then burns out, people who go door to door only to leave behind nothing but a prayer and a brochure. The longer you are active in relationships with people who are far from

God, the more they will believe you truly care about them, and the more they will open their lives to you. Your care can remind them that God is relational, drawing people into eternal relationship. To some extent, everyone joining Jesus in his mission is asking the question, "Is simple faithfulness enough?" I believe it is. Certainly fruitfulness is a secondary desire, and love will be our identifier (John 13:35), but yes, *faithfulness is enough*. Longevity will reveal faithfulness.

Like incarnation, longevity is not passive. I'm not just talking about existing in a place or relationship for a long time; longevity entails fighting through obstacles and road blocks to be the presence of Jesus to those around you because that is what God desires of us.

Ground-level connection. By its nature incarnation takes place in the trenches. Humans are designed for ground-level connection, and this is how we must minister on Jesus' behalf. There are no incarnational strategists, only practitioners. We can talk about incarnation and longevity all we want, but if we are avoiding the pain, joy, questions, and doubt of those around us, we fall short of faithfulness. The ordinary nature of the ground level is nearly the opposite of our culture of emotional highs and glorified social media updates. Living for Jesus in the trenches will lead you to some messy life situations, like the trench foot many soldiers acquired during World War I.

Ground-level connection is the hardest aspect of faithful presence to measure. We have all had seasons where we were disconnected from our neighbors, distracted from our mission, enamored of strategies when we should have been loving people. We often mistake busyness in ministry for joining the mission of God, and we equate much surface-level interaction with ministry success. But we see in Jesus' example—a firm commitment to be among rather than above, a lifelong connection to the same general area, and an authentic concern for the ground-level struggles of the people around him—that the soil where faith grows is richer in the trenches. The soil only gets richer the deeper we go.

There are no shortcuts to faithful presence. Eugene Peterson, a man I deeply respect, has lived decades of faithful presence among needy and ordinary people in local congregations. Late in his ministry he came to three realizations of how he would live the gospel patiently, locally, and personally.

> Patiently: I would stay with these people; there are no quick or easy ways to do this. Locally: I would embrace the conditions of this place—economics, weather, culture, schools, whatever—so that there would be nothing abstract or piously idealized about what I was doing. Personally: I would know them, know their names, know their homes, know their families, know their work.[3]

We must embrace these three if we are to live a faithful gospel.

Unfortunately, church leaders often communicate a value not of faithful presence but of its opposite. Jamie Arpin-Ricci, author of *Vulnerable Faith*, says that transience in church leaders communicates that place is inconsequential or unimportant. Even if lip service says otherwise, our actions speak louder. It might also communicate that the "goal" is to achieve the "suburban dream," feeding into the upwardly mobile culture.[4]

That's a good warning. I often hear about "carousel churches" that have a different lead pastor every year or two. In every case I have encountered, this has contributed to stagnancy and decline. How can sheep enjoy the pastures if their shepherds are distracted? Eugene Peterson grew up with a similar impression of pastors being disembodied from their places: "Pastor was an interim position on their way to some more celebrated work or exotic location."[5]

There are plenty of encouraging stories on the other side of the coin. My friend Scott returned to his hometown in the Denver metro area to plant a new church. He and his wife made the commitment to "stay when the cash runs out," to continue to minister to his hometown even if it leads him into undesirable work and unforeseen hardships. God has blessed their commitment to stay with deep trust among those in their church and lots of lost people giving their lives to Jesus.

I recently entered into a dialogue on hard topics with three other leaders who have made a commitment to our city. We want to be part of God's Kingdom breaking through right here in the midst of the challenges and wrongs of our city, and we want to do this together.

The notion of faithful presence sounds romantic at first.

But eventually the honeymoon stage ends, and just as in marriage, realities arise that you didn't read about in the books. Missiologist Paul Hiebert describes the process of a new place turning into our home.

> The realization dawns that this is now our home. Here our children will grow up as natives. And we must become one with these people with their unintelligible tongues and foreign ways before we can effectively share with them the Good News of the gospel. Suddenly, things that seemed romantic and exciting become strange and threatening.[6]

Hiebert calls this "the problem of cultural differences."[7] Cultural differences are present everywhere we go, but we adapt to them over time, and they shape our expectations for our next cross-cultural encounter. You may have already overcome some barriers to living in your community. You may have already learned the native tongue and rituals. You may have a hard time seeing past the cultural differences still in front of you. But you might be closer to breakthrough with people around you than you'd ever imagine.

OUTWARD MOBILITY

The draw away from place is largely rooted in consumption and illusion. We consume places and relationships as long as they are good for us: giving us a fuzzy feeling, making us happy, helping us live our dreams. We somehow believe in a kind of urban utopia, a hip, affordable, cultured, safe, neighborly place to live, requiring no sacrifice of us. Jonathan Wilson-Hartgrove says, "Intimacy without commitment is what society has traditionally called 'infidelity.'"[8] We must learn to battle through our infidelity to the places we reside and the people around us.

It's subtle, but it's pervasive. In the mid-twentieth century, large numbers of people moved out of urban areas to find their utopia—more square feet of property, less congestion, a greater feeling of safety, less traffic, and a better view of the horizon of the American Dream. In a culture where staying had been the norm, going became the new staying.

This suburban exodus had a broad cultural impact: communities where everyone looked alike (the phrase "white flight" is often used to describe the racial aspects of this phenomenon), longer commutes, more bills to pay, and less time with the family.

I live in one of those once-desirable, fifty-year-old suburban neighborhoods. People are no longer flocking to move to this once-dreamy section of the city. Today's moving patterns seem to be from ordinary places to notable places, but they are driven by eerily similar motivations to the "outward mobility" of that earlier era. Yesterday's suburban Shangri-las are today's forgotten neighborhoods. They aren't new enough to accommodate modern desires, but neither are they urban enough to be hip. Most cities I've observed are dotted with many such forgotten areas.

Think about the unintended consequences of these waves of relocation. We tend to think of commute time, but what about commute space? Interstate highways (which began construction in the midst of the suburban exodus) allow people to drive longer distances to work and recreation without thinking twice. Even if you drive fifteen minutes to work, you probably drive past whole neighborhoods, towns or cultural centers without even noticing. We become somehow numb when we cross that much space and pass through that many communities on the way to our places of work or play.

One consequence is that places no longer have their own significance; they are often thought of as just stops along the way. Hyper-mobility and addiction to technology are major factors that have led us to a feeling of placelessness and what Eugene Peterson calls "inhospitality."[9] Genuine rooted community gets sacrificed on the altar of upward and outward mobility. Friends might tell you, "Just gut it out for a few years, do your time, and see where the company will send you next." While it's certainly not sinful to move from one place to another, every rest stop on our journey makes us shout the question louder: "When will we be able to stop, unpack our bags, and settle in?"

I serve on a team that strategizes how to help improve some of the hard realities of my kids' school. The things elementary students are facing today are immense, but they can all be traced back to neglect. The school administration is wondering how they can get parents to nurture their kids, help them with homework, provide breakfast in the morning, pay attention to their relational needs, and encourage them to invest energy in school. Most of the problems schools are facing could be largely improved through simple nurture and investment. We can say the same thing of our communities.

THE OUTWARDLY MOBILE CHURCH

This distance from work, play, and friendships has not only affected North America's secular society; it's also affected the church. A pastor friend refers to the suburban communities between an urban core and its sprawling exurbs as "the donut." Most people focused on starting churches overlook these areas and the people dwelling in them. Many of the church buildings in these forgotten areas were built in the 1950s and 1960s; they were once bursting with possibilities, but those congregations have ceased to be a significant part of their neighborhoods. They could be incredibly strategic hubs to serve neighborhoods and deploy missionaries, if the church weren't so enthralled with the outward mobility of the age. Popular advice is to locate a new church near an interstate so people can quickly get in and get out, like they do at a stadium or a concert venue; such churches can effectively draw in many commuters, but their nearest neighbors are often an afterthought.

I like this idea from an older leader who launched new churches in my city for over fifty years: "For every church we are part of starting in a growing suburban area we should start one in an older urban area." This could bring a lot of balance to new churches in our cities instead of everyone heading to the same piece of ground. This man largely targeted the donut as a place to start new churches and practice faithful presence. He's asked the tough questions we all need to ask: how distance has accidentally disconnected us from one another and how our place factors into how we restore meaningful connection to our neighbors.

PRICED OUT OF GOD'S MISSION

Money is a real barrier to staying in your place. Financial stress attracts pastors to new, better-paying opportunities. They often feel they *can't* turn down a better salary in order to take better care of their family. Most pastors I meet have a desire to focus their efforts on leading a church full-time, but seminary debt pulls many people away from vocational ministry to better-paying opportunities.[10] I talk to a lot of young folks who want to go into the foreign mission field but are strapped with college debt. They sense any kind of ministry work will have to wait till midlife or the fourth quarter of their lives. We all know that vocation changes become harder later in our career, so these deferred plans for missions are likely taking people permanently out of the game. Many young leaders in my city are realizing mission can happen at home and are starting to kindle local, incarnational missions.

Jesus put on flesh and walked on dusty roads alongside sinful people, slowly building the first Christian community with no regular income and no place to lay his head (Luke 9:58). Incarnational mission involves becoming advocates, friends, listeners, caretakers, and shepherds of our communities. All these postures take time to germinate, and none of them is a direct path to prosperity. They all entail sacrifice. But all followers of Jesus are called to come and die with him if we are to experience true life with him. Can we reasonably expect to ascend to thrones of influence and impact without first descending to the cross with Jesus?

How would it change our churches if Christians committed to putting down roots in a community and staying? How would the influence of the local church change if we could honestly say we have no plan of leaving? If we lean hard into the promise that God will take care of his sheep—however untraditional, multi-vocational, or hard it might be?

Our places are suffering from the church's neglect. Many sectors and slices of our communities are untended, as the church seeks out greener pastures and its leaders struggle to keep up with an outwardly mobile lifestyle. As we Christians have kept pace with the cultural neglect of place, we have too often neglected our communities—the urgent conversations and harsh realities around us. Physical neglect is easy to spot in a community, but spiritual neglect can hollow out a place. We cannot leave our communities as orphans to fend for themselves; to embrace God's mission is to offer our place the love, nurture, respect, and direction it so desperately needs.

WHERE IS HOME?

I am a former model. Believe it or not, this statement is true. My mom signed me up for a few shows at a local J.C. Penney store when I was a kid so I could get free school clothes. I still can't believe she made me do that. So, technically it's true that I have had a modeling career. But that one truth could never be considered the full truth about me.

"Home isn't a place," I hear people say. "Home can be a person, a journey, or memories you take with you." This is true in a way, similar to how "everyone is my neighbor" is true. But it's not the full truth. Even as we wax eloquent about how we can go anywhere in a global society, we wonder at our feelings of lostness, our growing sense of disconnection. There's still a longing for home deep within us.

I missed the boat on the importance of home for years. Colorado Springs was where I lived, but it wasn't my home. I had an address where my mail arrived, but I carried no local weight that drew me into responsibility. I had an escape plan; I even tried to carry it out a few times. For a season my wife and I investigated planting a church in Boulder, Colorado. It seemed more desirable, more noble, weirder (in a good way) than where we were. But as we walked the ground and prayed we knew God was calling Colorado Springs home for us.

It's okay to be homeless, rootless, for a while. It's okay to not have a thirty-year plan. But Christ-followers should be a gift to their neighborhood, and a church should be a gift to its city.[11] And maintaining an escape plan makes that impossible. In his book *Incarnate* Michael Frost says, "Christians should be the most rooted people in their community; their loyalty and devotion to a particular geographical area and everyone who lives there should be legendary."[12] I dream of a day when churches regain legendary status in their cities.

A friend of mine is a pastor in Colorado Springs. He's bivocational; his primary job is as a firefighter. That work led him into the sphere of public health, where he noticed a crack in our city: many ill people could not obtain crucial prescription drugs. My friend's church decided to start a pharmacy and a health clinic, something that had never been attempted by a church here. They have helped countless people obtain expensive meds and have helped other churches start similar hubs of hope in their cities. I would call this type of ministry legendary.

Earlier this year my family had a huge rollaway dumpster delivered to our driveway. We had accumulated a well-hidden stash of junk on the side of our home we referred to as "our dirty secret," and it was finally time to do something about it. Twice during that week neighbors stopped me; they were concerned that we were moving. I took it as a compliment: *They actually care if we stay! They don't want us to move!* We were no longer a rock with no moss. We were locals. We were incarnational. We were faithfully present.

QUESTIONS FOR REFLECTION AND DISCUSSION

Would anyone care if you put a For Sale sign in your yard? Would the businesses, residents, and organizations around your church building care if your church relocated?

How can you work to gain a winsome reputation in your community? How might a commitment to place lead to more opportunities for gospel witness?

What simple acts of care could you regularly undertake to bring wholeness back to your community?

① IDEA OF HAVING A DUMPSTER DELIVERED & INVITING NEIGHBORS TO "SPRING CLEAN"

2

BIKES, GARDENS, AND FORGOTTEN PLACES

"The twentieth-century American dream was to move out and move up. The twenty-first-century dream seems to be to put down deeper roots."

RICHARD FLORIDA, URBAN STUDIES THEORIST

"This notion of place, a return to become more rooted and established, with a heightened sense of localism is certainly not a conversation exclusive to the church."

SEAN BENESH, *VESPAS, CAFÉS, SINGLESPEED BIKES, AND URBAN HIPSTERS*

As is the case with most great things, one of my favorite traditions happened by accident. We tripped over it and immediately knew it was worth its weight in gold. My dad, my brother, and I had booked tickets to visit my grandfather one more time before he passed away, but his health faded more quickly than we anticipated. In just two weeks we had planned and performed his funeral ceremony, and we were all back in our own towns grieving his loss. Due to the nightmare of ticket changes, we couldn't get our money back or change the location to someplace more desirable. We were left with tickets to a very normal Midwestern city we had all been to before. Instead of changing the tickets, my dad, my brother, and I decided to keep our plane flights, fly to that city, and make a weekend of it. We would treat it as an urban retreat and city immersion. If I'm being honest, part of me wondered, "Is this place worth our time?"

We found ourselves wandering the city with no real plan. We strolled through city blocks and discovered local hangouts. We stopped at unique places and talked with strangers. Locals were thrilled to recommend their favorite spots. We found amazing things we didn't know existed.

A very ordinary city came alive to us. There were exciting things happening here!

This has turned into an annual tradition we call "City a Year." Each year we pick a different underrated city and immerse ourselves in it. Although these are not "hot cities" with the clout of New York or San Francisco, they are teeming with life—people who have decided to make it their home and celebrate its uniqueness. We listen to stories from the locals, travel by foot and two wheels, and choose our food based on local recommendations. I've learned through these adventures that an undercurrent of urban recovery is happening everywhere. We have to slow down long enough to see the beauty of our places instead of just a dot on a map or a road to another place. If you're not looking for it, you won't find it.

UNDER-UNDERSTANDING CITIES

While I don't claim to be an expert on cities and their complexities, there are three crucial aspects to understanding them.

City as geography and landscape. Cities are located in a particular place with a particular geography. They take up space somewhere, they grow larger and taller with more inhabitants, or shorter and smaller as people leave. The ground they sit on has experienced a lot of history and a lot of change. Port cities, Midwestern cities, and cities next to mountains all have distinct cultures, rhythms, and patterns shaped in part by their geography.

The idea of cities as *simply* geography and landscape, however, is probably the biggest under-understanding of cities. Some of the best cities to visit are hard to get to; their greatness is obscured by an unpleasant climate, or overlooked in favor of cities with better views. As simply a geographical space, they don't measure up, regardless of how amazing the local culture may be. Even popular cities, however, suffer the neglect of their visitors; tourists flock to spectacular architecture or natural wonders, driving right past spectacular people and creative contributions in the process. Cities are much more than places.

City as a web of relationships. In any particular city, thousands of relational webs exist. These relationships can generate great ideas, innovation, and collaboration. Each week I seem to uncover a different web of relationships in my city, from business bureaus to civic clubs to war veterans to golfing buddies. Don't be fooled: people are what truly makes cities great. Mapping the webs of relationships—the subcultures—can help us understand the potential for the gospel to travel through a city and impact its different sectors. These webs are people groups, and to put this into global missions lingo, our cities have many unreached people groups residing right in front of our faces. Some speak different languages, some speak just like we do, but all of them need Jesus.

City as a blank canvas. The longer we are active in cities the more potential for creation and innovation we see. I talk with people almost every week who have ideas and dreams for our city, from business development to community spaces to taking care of the down and out. Perhaps this is because of the innate potential cities have for new creation. In Revelation 21 the image of a new heaven and a new earth is found in the image of a city. City renewal can actually be a missiological and theological statement!

Through human connection and interaction, new creations arise, and our love for our cities can grow. Abandoned warehouses turn into retail spaces; forgotten urban neighborhoods become desirable to live in again. There is no limit to the creativity that can germinate in cities. When churches get inordinately focused on taking care of their own people, they lose creativity; but when churches are focused on the world outside their doors, they gain access to the creative potential of their city.

LOCALIZING

Our world is localizing again. While I'm not attempting to give a sociologist's perspective, gas prices, the rise of local craft commerce, a cultural exhaustion from suburban sprawl, and urban frontierism all contribute to the rediscovery of locality. Cities are no longer just growing out; they're growing up. Warehouses from a bygone industrial era are becoming hubs for commerce and habitation, and one-story homes are being razed to build five-story lofts.

Local connection is on the rise again. Farmers markets providing local produce are popping up everywhere. "Share boxes" in neighborhoods are a visible sign people want to connect with others around them and repurpose unneeded stuff. Posters with the mantra "Buy Local" plaster the windows of shops and restaurants. There is a rebirth of nearness in relationships, physical space, food, commerce, and even church community. Young families are longing for intergenerational relationships with their older neighbors. Café owners and makers of goods are seeking to source their ingredients as locally as possible. Many folks who used to drive great distances to work and play are peering over handlebars and wearing a helmet instead of a seatbelt. Cities are alive again; the once-blank canvas is bursting with color.

The people of Jesus must anticipate opportunities brought on by this cultural shift. The ground is prepped and the harvest is ready for a rooted, connected, and local focus to mission. People are hungry to know neighbors again and push past the awkwardness to see each other's souls up close.

Your neighbors might deny this. But I bet they want you to connect with them. What if Christians were bold enough to take the first step of engaging local relationships? What if churches were as serious about local renewal as the entrepreneurs in our cities?

EXILED

The words of Jeremiah 29 are often quoted in dark moments when longing for a bright future. The prophet Jeremiah pens these words to a dejected and exiled Judah. Nebuchadnezzar had exiled them to Babylon. This wasn't exactly their dream. I can imagine how abandoned and pushed aside they felt. The words of this passage are surprising and have much to teach us.

> Thus says the LORD of hosts, the God of Israel,
> to all the exiles whom I have sent into exile from
> Jerusalem to Babylon: Build houses and live in them;
> plant gardens and eat their produce. Take wives and
> have sons and daughters; take wives for your sons,
> and give your daughters in marriage, that they may
> bear sons and daughters; multiply there, and do
> not decrease. But seek the welfare of the city where
> I have sent you into exile, and pray to the LORD
> on its behalf, for in its welfare you will find your
> welfare.   JEREMIAH 29:4-7

The first time I read Jeremiah 29 through the lens of my city I was blown away. I felt like an exile. I hadn't taken the time to cultivate spiritual gardens. I thought my city wasn't ripe enough for the kind of ministry I was called to. I poked fun at my city as I believed it wasn't cultured enough to enjoy living in. I was not praying for God's work in my city; I was busy wishing I could be somewhere else. I wasn't working for its welfare; I was making a list of all the reasons I should leave.

Prayer walking has helped to move me from a posture of exile to a posture of cultivation. I started going on prayer walks with leaders from different sectors of our city. I let church planters and community leaders become my guides; they showed me the physical geography and helped me understand what realities to pray for. As we walked and prayed, I came to understand God's invitation to partner with him in the renewing of our places.

My wife and I are committed to raising our family in the heart of the good, bad, and ugly of our city. This isn't always easy, as we push through our disappointment and feelings of wanting to be somewhere else. Each week seems to be a recalibration of the risk of staying present and engaged. It's about fighting the impulse to disengage and simply staying committed to keep showing up and loving people. It's about fighting the impulse to dream of how life would be better where the grass seems greener, safer, or more cultured.

I'm not trying to give a false reality that you will feel a romance for your city all the time. A lot of people feel like they are in exile. You may be one of them. There are always people who wish they didn't live where they've ended up. Recently I was speaking at a church on Jeremiah 29. After sharing this passage I asked, "Who feels like they are in exile in our city?" Several people raised their hands. We had a powerful time of prayer as we gathered around exiles and prayed for God to show them contentment and opportunity right here.

THE RIGHT VENUE

Perhaps you have heard the phrase, "They are so heavenly minded that they are no earthly good." For many this phrase defines the church in North America. On the whole, Christians are not seen as advocates for the suffering; we're not seen as champions of the beauty around us.

Growing up in a college town, I was always told college students are the ultimate free riders. They carry the stigma of being disengaged from their local context. They are known for consuming places. I have always loved college students, however, and I believe they have a high potential to become local missionaries. For example, for the last two years a student who is part of our missional community has been faithfully cultivating relationships with local artists as only a college student could do. Fellow artists became her mission field as she worked in different media to reach people's souls.

I went to an event where my friend and her fellow senior art majors summed up their four years of study by sharing their portfolios. I absolutely loved the evening! Every single presentation carried a strong theme of place. They were all required to do art residencies with families in their homes, making unique art for their host families. One student did an art walk, leading people to different houses to see and discuss the art displayed in each home. Other students did sidewalk chalk projects; I almost cried thinking of their masterpieces being washed away during the next rainstorm.

Each presenter wanted his or her art to change and impact others. Students sat in parks with signs inviting passers-by to ask questions. With the beautiful mountain backdrop, some students would decorate a hiking trail with various installments of art. Walls, sidewalks, living rooms, paths, parks, and neighborhoods replaced galleries, the more conventional setting for fine art; these localized spaces allowed the students' creativity to thrive. These art students had become cultivators of human connection and local space; they inspired new possibilities in me and the others who attended.

One student lamented "the hard jump to the gallery," the inevitability of their artwork moving from living rooms to neutral public spaces. None of the students seemed to be enthusiastic about the idea of getting their art into a gallery, although most acknowledged that it seemed like the right next step in their art career. I'm in no way saying, however, that God is not at work in the galleries and stages of life. In fact, art galleries can themselves become reflecting ponds for God's work in a city. In the same way that artists can localize their work in a way that blesses real people in their real lives, galleries can showcase the distinct gifts and perspectives of their locality. In that way, an art gallery can be a blessing to its city.

A church in my city has ministered through art since they launched. They narrowed their focus to spend much of their effort engaging and participating in the artist subculture in our city. They're not trying to be trendy; it's just who they are. Desiring to deepen their connection to the arts community, they opened the Rooted Studio: four members of their congregation, working in media ranging from the visual arts to hairstyling, became artists in residence. They moved their church offices there and fitted it for a small music venue and a place to host art shows. This church has intentionally invited a mix of people who know Jesus and people who don't to create a hub for excellent art and meaningful interaction.

A church's property, its space, can be a significant local venue. It might not be an art studio; it could be a space for mechanics, an aftercare program, a food pantry, a community meeting space, a dog park, a coffee shop, or a home for kids aging out of foster care. There is an endless list of unique ideas that can connect people to God and others. Don't try to copy another church in another community; do the hard work of contextualizing to the cracks in your community. Growing roots in the subcultures you are called to reach will increase your ability to relate to people and reach them.

As followers of Jesus who are tasked with bringing the salty flavor and glow of the best news ever to those around us, we must fight the temptation to look elsewhere—to galleries, stages, or cities already in the limelight—as the obvious setting for the work of God. God is already working right before our eyes, in homes, on sidewalks, in parks, and in third places. Our task is to recognize where God is working, and join in.[1]

OLD PLACES, NEW GROWTH

The American Dream is changing. Instead of just settling in big homes in the suburbs, many people are being drawn back to cities. More people are living in older homes and relying on bikes for transportation. Today old-brick urban spaces are hot, and there is only so much to go around, so people settle for less square footage in their homes in exchange for a closer proximity to public schools, shopping, and parks. Bikes aren't just transportation; they are an expression of a new local, community-centered mind-set.

Gardens have made a massive resurgence. Parks, organizations, and churches are hosting community gardens. Raised beds are popping up in front yards and urban spaces that were once oceans of cracked concrete. People everywhere are experiencing the work of cultivation and the joy of the harvest. We are in process of launching a community garden at the local elementary school through a partnership of churches. Teachers, students, and neighbors will plant, tend, and harvest these gardens, with the produce going straight to the lunchroom.

For the past few years I have been drawn to the story of Braddock, Pennsylvania. Braddock is a recovering steel town near Pittsburgh. In the height of the industrial revolution it was booming and touted as the place to be. They once said, "If Braddock doesn't have it, you don't need it."[2] With the crash of steel in the Monongahela Valley, however, the town hit an all-time low. People lost jobs and left. The city has lost many buildings to the landfill and is trying to figure out how to utilize the forgotten places in town.

On a one-day immersion into the real life of Braddock, we visited with several community leaders, including the curator of Andrew Carnegie's first library, local artists, and a small business owner. The most inspiring person we met was Marshall Hart, the lead caretaker of Braddock Farms. As we pulled up to a once-abandoned space, we saw a beautiful garden on both sides of the street, rife with vegetables and fruits, with giant smokestacks and a steel mill on its border. A few people were hard at work, their heads down close to the soil.

Sitting with Marshall and listening to his story was better than reading a book on gardening. He came to Braddock several years ago through a gardening and urban renewal program, and has dedicated this season of his life to compiling compost and tilling the plants that grow in rich urban soil. I asked Marshall why urban gardening is on the rise; he noted how powerful it is to look after ourselves in an increasingly outsourced world. "Gardening is something we have been doing for so long," he said, "that it is imprinted somewhere within us. Growing connects us to the world that we often forget we are completely reliant on and a part of."

Gardening is fun for Marshall, but it also connects him to the natural world, and to his neighbors. "Some of the best people I've met are gardeners. Really, the question is, how could I not be passionate about it?" He shared the impact of their rubble pile turned urban sanctuary. "Braddock Farms has become an important part of the community for a large handful of people, a place not only to get food, but to talk across the fence, a place that many of the children in the borough visit over and over as they grow up. It's a point of pride."

I admire how Marshall is doing what he loves in a hard

place. Through simple faithfulness to this task, he has been part of turning a food desert into a town that supplies local produce to feed those in need. He has helped to foster a gathering space people are proud of. By doing his part he is changing the narrative of Braddock.

Gardens put us in our place. They literally ground us. And that ground can become a place of redemption. Abandoned and fallow places can become vibrant, cultivated places of provision. This is the narrative of redemption. It's no accident that we find gardens throughout Scripture. The Bible starts in a rural garden and ends in an urban garden. Gardens represent a redemptive return to divine partnership; they remind of us God's creative and provisional work. When I stand with my kids at the edge of a community garden in my neighborhood, built by an older church, I see the beauty of God's diverse and creative touch. As Paul writes, "We are [God's] workmanship, created in Christ Jesus for good works, which God prepared beforehand, that we should walk in them" (Ephesians 2:10). A garden can remind us that we are built in the image of the great cultivator to cultivate things.

Paul speaks about our role in cultivation in his first letter to the Corinthians.

What, after all, is Apollos? And what is Paul? Only servants, through whom you came to believe—as the Lord has assigned to each his task. I planted the seed, Apollos watered it, but God has been making it grow. So neither the one who plants nor the one who waters is anything, but only God, who makes things grow. The one who plants and the one who waters have one purpose, and they will each be rewarded according to their own labor. For we are coworkers in God's service; you are God's field, God's building.

1 CORINTHIANS 3:5-9, NIV

Cultivation of any kind will require four things: participation, partnership, patience, and produce. Without any of these, a garden is just a pile of dirt and our life of mission is just a life of busy disappointment. These four things are also markers along our journey toward cultivating faithful presence.

Participation. Paul reminds us we all have a task in cultivating the gospel. Gardening looks easy when you're watching others harvest their vegetables. It might even look dreamy, hip, and vogue to fill a basket of harvested goods. Composting, tilling soil, planting seeds, and weeding are different. They aren't exactly leisure activities, but we are shaped through them.

Cultivation of any kind takes hard work that can bring great satisfaction. Many Friday mornings I don't want to roll out of bed to brew coffee and spend time with my neighbors. It might be snowy or rainy outside, or I might be craving that one day to sleep in. A ministry of longevity requires us to stay engaged and just keep showing up to participate in God's ongoing work. Participation in God's mission in relationships, neighborhoods, and cities will take commitment.

Partnership. Paul reminds us we partner with God and others in ministry. True gardeners realize without sun and water and rich soil, they'll have no crops. In ministry, especially a ministry of patience, we must learn our place as partners in God's mission to redeem all things. Gardening solo is not much fun. We must learn to partner with other people to serve the common good. We must become masters of building bridges and finding common ground so we can partner with organizations, neighbors, coworkers, and friends to have a blessing presence on everyone around us. If you start looking for partners you will find dedicated people who already have a reputation for loving and serving your city.

Patience. Paul reminds us the gospel is a seed and will take time to grow. If you ask most urban and suburban kids today, "Where do your fruits and vegetables come from?" they will likely answer, "The grocery store." We go to the store and it's ready, and we feel inconvenienced just to wait in the checkout line!

In a world of immediacy, we fall into the same posture in our discipleship. We want things fast. Most of us have the impulse to go and conquer, and if we don't see results quickly, our eyes wander to the next place. We lack the patience to wait on God's work. Gardening is hard work, and spiritual gardening is no exception. There is no way around patience on the journey to faithful presence.

Produce. Paul reminds us only God can make things grow. Scripture is clear: good trees bear good fruit (Matthew 7:18). When you are faithful in a place, God develops the fruits of the Spirit in you, and he will also use you to impact others. People will take notice of the fruit of your life and ask questions. God might not bring spiritual conversions, or gather large crowds around you, or have others thank you for your faithful presence, but Scripture doesn't promise any of these. If we are going to choose to plant spiritual gardens, we will have no choice but to trust God, and God alone, to bring fruit from our investment in the lives of those around us. Through the process of staying present and engaged, I have found that people are not only open to spiritual conversations but intrigued when Christians are visible and active in their communities.

The most physically redemptive work I have experienced happened through the dreams of an incredible woman I met in Saint Louis. I was leading a group of folks to partner with a church there in their mission to serve their neighbors. They weren't putting on a show for us; they were inviting us into their rhythms of caring for their place and the people who called it home. A small team of us sat on a front porch with Ms. Lovie. She reminded us of the Oracle from *The Matrix*, so we all listened up to whatever wisdom she dished out.

Ms. Lovie told us the story of how her neighborhood had changed from a thriving community to a rundown and unsafe place. The brick house on the corner had long since been condemned; everyone in the neighborhood knew it had become a crack house, the portal for drugs to enter their community. As Ms. Lovie would look across the street at the house and pray for God's work in the neighborhood, she made God a promise: "If you take that house down, I'll build a garden there."

Not too long after that prayer, the city commissioned workers to demolish the house and cart off the rubble. All that was left was an empty plot of land—perfect for a garden. A local church brought teams in to move soil and build raised beds, following Ms. Lovie's directions. Today this former crack house site is a beautiful green space; kids in a rough neighborhood are growing and eating their own produce. What was once the disgrace of the neighborhood is now a space for everyone to enjoy.

Imagine if Ms. Lovie had looked out on her changing neighborhood and decided to leave before it got too bad. Imagine if her frustration had caused her to give up. Imagine if instead of losing its crack house, that neighborhood lost its Ms. Lovie. It was because she chose to stay, because she chose to build something good rather than resign herself to something bad or escape to something better, that Ms. Lovie was able to lead her neighborhood into a new, redemptive future.

THE RETURN OF THE FRONT PORCH

From the same spot she watches over the neighborhood garden, Ms. Lovie gave me master's-level teaching on the front porch. I watched relationships unfold as she helped us map the interactions on her street. She began to talk about the relationships she cultivates from right there in her chair on the front porch. People asked to borrow things, and one family invited a friend over for a cookout that night. One man offered to mow another neighbor's lawn. People weren't hiding in their backyards, but lingering on the "median space" of their front porches. It was refreshing and intriguing.

There is a resurgence of spaces and places that spur us back toward one another. The old television show *Cheers* created a vision for a place "where everybody knows your name," and that vision is happening in many cafés, coffee shops, parks, and neighborhoods today. Joseph Myers, in his book *The Search to Belong*, says that the contemporary hunger for median space

> may arise from the recent history of minimizing the importance of these relationships. Median spaces are the spaces that include our social and personal connections. Median spaces are where people experience "front porch." Front porches are significant to our experience of community and belonging.[3]

Like many people, we don't have a front porch. Our home was built with the assumption that homeowners wanted privacy, so the backyard is optimized for outdoor activities, and the front of the house is relatively uninviting. Instead of simply spending time in our backyard, however, we created a few small rocked areas in the front yard with a café table and lounge chairs to be visible to those walking by. When the weather is nice I try to stay outside as school gets out and linger at the table next to our house; kids end up playing, and parents end up talking. With a little imagination, our street, sidewalk, and front yard have become median space.

I believe Christians can be both active participants and known characters in our places and spaces. Perhaps you will have to fight off some of the very fears my family wrestles through. When we are faithful and intentional in median spaces, we are reinforcing the story of a faithful and present God. When relationships begin to feel like extended families, our neighbors are welcomed into God's story, where they can "taste and see that the LORD is good" (Psalm 34:8). When we invite others a step deeper into our lives, our dinner tables tell the story of a banquet feast we will enjoy together in heaven.[4] How we live out compassion to the misfits, the ordinaries, and the outcasts around us tells the story of our great adoptive Father. How we conduct our lives is what others will believe about God. Nearly every Christ follower I meet has great intentions to love others around them, but nearly every Christ follower I meet is struggling to meaningfully connect with people who don't know Jesus. Perhaps our communities need to focus more on meaningfully hanging out in median spaces. Myers asks:

> How do we invite strangers into the family? How can we help with the experience of belonging? How do we develop healthy community? I believe the answers may be found somewhere in the median spaces—somewhere on the front porch.[5]

Paul shares to the church at Ephesus the truth that God has brought us in as family. "You are no longer strangers and aliens, but you are fellow citizens with the saints and members of the household of God" (Ephesians 2:19). We have opportunities every day to fold people into our lives, to call them from the front porch spaces to the table, as a sign they are welcome in our lives and families.

There is a hunger for relationships in our culture. This hunger is leading many people out of hiding and back into median spaces. The question is not whether connection is happening in our cities, but rather how Christians will join this movement.

QUESTIONS FOR REFLECTION AND DISCUSSION

How are you praying for your city? In what ways are you seeking its welfare?

What median spaces can you and your family be faithfully present in? How will you make faithful presence a discipline?

What space is your community longing for that you can provide, curate, or inhabit?

THE STORY BEHIND YOUR PLACE

"Where you invest your love, you invest your life."
MUMFORD AND SONS, "AWAKE MY SOUL"

"If you don't know history, then you don't know anything. You are a leaf that doesn't know it is part of a tree."
MICHAEL CRICHTON

"Maybe the world breaks on purpose so we can have work to do. People think there aren't frontiers anymore. They can't see how frontiers are all around us."
"TO WORK," A COMMERCIAL FOR LEVI'S JEANS

I LIVE IN AN older house. When we moved in, my wife and I easily overlooked its character—its classic designs and unique floor plans—and immediately saw the things we wanted to change and update. We have done a good bit of updating, but we have also come to appreciate the work of previous owners: a beautiful addition that has become the lifeblood of the home, countless rosebushes, and an amazing patio area. When people tell us how much they love our home, we are quick to praise the previous owners for the time, energy, and money they poured into it.

Rumor has it my neighborhood used to be an apple orchard, and in our yard are two towering apple trees that produce great apples and cider for us in the fall. The previous owners made a decision not to cut the trees down. We get to enjoy the fruit of trees we didn't plant.

Spiritually speaking, we all get to eat from gardens we didn't plant. In the Gospel of John we find Jesus lifting the disciples' eyes to the harvest. "I sent you to reap that for which you did not labor," he tells them. "Others have labored, and you have entered into their labor" (John 4:38). This doesn't seem very fair. Sometimes I've wondered why God didn't show me more fruit for my labors; other times I've wondered why he has let me experience the fruit of work others have done. I'm not alone: This is a good day in many pockets of the North American church. We get to experience new ministry models, new understandings of the role of pastors, new vision for Christian laypeople, and new church start-ups. Most of this newness comes to us as a result of the hard work of people who paved the way before us so we could travel on it more smoothly.

There are spiritual leaders and churches in your area who might not be thriving right now, but who have been plowing gospel ground for years in your community. The individuals and churches who came before us prayed for the people in our cities, walked its ground, and pointed people to Jesus long before we did. They experienced challenges we will never know. That deserves honor.

Recently I was in a Colorado mountain town consulting with leaders of a church who were trying to unify and reach people again. The church had spiraled to a point where they appeared to be heading toward their death bed. I noticed a small plaque outside the church building, right next to the front door, and jotted down a few names from it. I did some research and found out that the founder's heart had been broken for miners giving their lives to the gold rush. He wanted them to chase the glory of God instead of the riches of prospecting. I stood in awe, thinking about how God had used this man in mining camps to share about Jesus, send out new missionaries to the miners, and establish local churches in unreached towns all over the western United States. This church was planted accidentally, the outgrowth of a man's desires to make Jesus known in the hard places. After I shared this history with the church's leaders, they gained a renewed respect for the heritage and story of their church, a better understanding of their present situation, and a vision for shaping the future.

THE PAST BEHIND YOUR PRESENT

I lived in our neighborhood two years before I heard about "the incident." I was talking to an older gentleman who used to live in our neighborhood twenty years prior. I began to ask him questions and try to piece some things together. Everything in this neighborhood was laid out with community and connection in mind. Initially the neighborhood was designed to funnel parents and kids to the school and the park right next to it. There were common walkways between homes where kids could safely walk to school without having to cross streets. A church was even started across the street from the school to reach a growing parish.

My new friend told me that kids used to flock to school each morning via the throughways instead of taking a bus—until they were fenced up and closed off. One morning a man exposed himself to kids as they were coming down the throughway between the fences. The kids ran back to their homes, the neighborhood went on high alert for the predator, and the kids were told not to use the throughways again. Before long they were all boarded up.

Now I understood some of the little deaths my neighbors have grieved for years. In a moment my neighborhood traded connectedness for suspicion. The flow of life in the neighborhood had been completely changed by one idiot.

Every neighborhood has cracks in it. The pain is real, but it might take some work to uncover it. The cracks show the brokenness of our world and expose the skepticism and distrust that has trumped neighborliness in our day. If we are going to be part of renewing our places, we must take on the posture of gospel sociologists, community investigators, and missiologists seeking to uncover the cracks so we can illuminate Jesus there. Instead of entering our places with solutions, we need to come asking important questions about its past. As Jon Huckins and Jon Hall put it: "What's the local history and how does that inform the neighborhood's current reality?"[1]

I hope a guy wouldn't go on a first date and talk the whole time. The goal of a first date is to get to know someone, and asking questions is a way of showing respect. A new community is like a first date: you don't know this place yet, and you need to show it respect. A missionary approach to a place should follow this order:

STORY OF A PLACE → CURRENT REALITIES → NEEDS → MINISTRY STRATEGY

Listen to the story of your place from people who care about it. Ponder how the story of your place has led to its current realities. From those current realities will emerge a list of needs, and those needs can determine your ministry strategy.

One of the greatest ministry mistakes we make is forming strategy without properly understanding the past story and current realities. A soup kitchen, biking club, or coffee shop might work in one place, but it might not be meeting actual community needs in another. We must take on the posture of curious question askers instead of problem solvers if we desire to have long-term impact in our places.

THE PEOPLE BEHIND MY NEIGHBORHOOD

When we moved into our neighborhood we saw cars, houses, and yards. We saw a pleasant neighborhood with nicely manicured lawns, mildly friendly people, and a traffic jam twice a day around the start and end of the school day. It took living there for almost a year before we began to see the cracks.

People were disconnected—dare I say, lonely? Many neighbors wrestling with serious health issues had no close connections. People were embarrassed about the weeds overwhelming their lawns. Parents ignored one another as each dropped their kids off at school and picked them back up again. People were coexisting but simply weren't engaging each other.

This is when things got real. We could choose to acknowledge those cracks or pretend they didn't exist.

We decided to throw a block party. *Why not try to meet everyone in one fell swoop*, I thought. My wife and I hoped it would help to hear their stories and see how connected they were to each other. We had no idea who was coming, but our missional community had seeded the night with people to create the atmosphere, man the grill, and hopefully break the awkwardness.

On the night of the block party, people we had never seen were walking up the street with Tupperware as old as eight-tracks. We formally opened the block party by introducing ourselves, and I asked, "Have you ever had a block party before?"

Someone yelled, "We used to do them every year. The last one was in '88."

I was blown away that no one had taken the initiative to throw a simple block party in more than twenty years!

The block party was an incredible introduction to people we call friends today. Our neighborhood is completely ordinary, yet completely unique, filled with an unlikely cast of characters who have shaped our lives in our neighborhood.

"Two-Dollar Bill" is the patriarch and busybody of the neighborhood. He slips a two-dollar bill in my hand at every Free Coffee Friday. I stopped trying to avoid his drug-deal handshakes after three weeks. Although he always seems upbeat and busy with friends, his brother, best friend, and next-door neighbor died the year we moved in. It's tearing him up inside.

Dan and Jamie have become dear friends. We shared almost every Denver Bronco football game together for two seasons, and we still watch many of the games together. They helped watch our kids and we helped watch theirs. We started the tradition of game night on each of our birthdays. They began to talk to us about how they were exiting the Mormon faith, and we were glad to listen and support them in their exodus. They have come to our church gathering to hear me preach and watched our babies get dedicated. We grieved the day they moved six miles away, but living next door to one another brought us together, and we still meet up with them occasionally.

On the other side of us lives an elderly couple, Charlie and Jean, who love our kids to pieces. They have given my kids enough powdered donuts and cracker packs to feed villages. It's not uncommon for our kids to make multiple trips to their house each day. Charlie and Jean have lived in the neighborhood for thirty-four years and have been through several serious health issues since we've lived here. Charlie is the self-appointed welcomer when people move into the neighborhood. When I ask my three-year-old son, "Who is your best friend?" he says, "Charlie is." I think it's pretty cool that his best friend is over eighty, and so does Charlie.

Sue works the night shift. Neighbors rarely see her. People had pegged her as "the cold-hearted, kid-unfriendly one," and neighbors warned us about it. Turns out she loves kids; a medical professional, she specializes in emergency medical calls for kids. Sue not only gave us permission to use the edge of her property for Free Coffee Friday, but she offered to bring cinnamon rolls. Sue reminds us that many people around us are not as they seem.

At the block party, Larita and Arch shared about the two children they have lost. They lost one to suicide many years ago. They started a local support group for parents who have lost children to suicide. Now it's an international nonprofit with hundreds of chapters. I would have never known the nice older guy watering his grass has affected thousands of lives all over the world. Once a neighborhood tragedy, Larita and Arch's work has become the pride of the neighborhood.

I need to share about one woman, the one forceful opponent of community in our neighborhood. As if the "No trespassing, violators will be prosecuted" sign wasn't clear enough, she took the time to walk a flyer for our upcoming block party back to our house and slap it on our door. I'm not sure why, but right now she doesn't want to live in a neighborhood; she wants to live in a house. I've learned not to take it personally, just to pray for her. Occasionally you will come across this reality in neighborhoods. People have experienced pain, and when you get close enough you simply can't avoid it.

Loren and Gina are a great couple dedicating their lives to serving two live-in special-needs adults. While he was in recovery, Loren came to know Jesus. Gina feels the freedom to come over and ask to borrow things or get advice from my wife. Eric, one of the special-needs adults in their home—a 6'5" twenty-four-year-old functioning as a kid—was bounced around through foster care growing up; Loren and Gina's house has become his longest stay in any one home. He comes over to our house a lot to play with our kids and hang out with our family. We were just approved as "natural caretakers" for Eric so we can occasionally give his host parents a break.

The other people on our street include a single real estate agent, a recluse, someone experiencing serious bipolar disorder, an adult who has never been able to move out of their parents' home, and some very successful business owners. I would guess my neighborhood is representative of all neighborhoods; every neighborhood has diversity, brokenness, beauty, stories—and most of all, untapped potential.

It's easy to bypass the deep connection we can find right where we live. By focusing on a small sphere of influence we can actually have a much deeper and wider impact. The authors of the book *The New Parish* put the challenge before us: "Are you a character in the story of your neighborhood?"[2] We must move beyond being observers and reporters in our places to become characters and contributors; as we do so, we come to appreciate the characters around us.

TELLING AN ALTERNATIVE STORY

People have always complained about there not being enough culture and art in my city. Many people have left, believing the ground was infertile and couldn't produce the harvest of culture, economics, and diversity they were looking for. When I encounter this complaint I ask, "Would you be willing to stay and cultivate a more robust culture here?" Often people are willing to stay and dig in, but they have never been challenged to do so.

Ironically, our city is far more diverse and cultured than many places. But people want to experience a perfect culture they have idealized or a snapshot they've romanticized from a magazine. They are thinking of the ten most cultured neighborhoods in the ten best cities in America, and our city can't compete with the highlight images of others places we've seen on social media.

Objectifying cities for what they can offer us is a kind of "pornography of place," a fantasy that simply isn't realistic. Like an angry teenager with identity issues, we naively lift our eyes to other places, other churches, other community groups, and other relationships, believing somehow it would be better to live anywhere but here. People looking for utopia miss the good things developing right in front of them.

To help tell an alternative story, my wife and I started a small company called Stay Forth Designs. The first T-shirt we produced says "I Dig Colorado Springs." We gave shirts to people who are working for the good of our city. We are creating similar visible goods to encourage rootedness in other communities, no matter how bleak the reputation. My wife and I believe branding and living a new message of places has the power to transform attitudes and actions. It's important to recognize when your city has a stigma against it; there is incredible power when people discover a common love for their place.

One of my favorite examples of telling an alternative story is unfolding in Pueblo, Colorado, a city built on the steel industry. People often refer to Pueblo as "the armpit of Colorado." Calling itself The Pearl, a church moved to a broken-down part of town, renting a grungy old bar they call The Beard. When I walked in for a tour, we woke up Mike, a homeless man who lives there and "keeps on eye on the place." The Pearl hosts concerts there, ranging from hip-hop to folk, that draw a diverse cross-section of the community.

The Pearl has a vision to help change the narrative of the city. Whenever and however they can express it, their message is, "We love Pueblo." As I drove around town with one of the pastors, he told me their greatest need is for vibrant Christians to choose to stay. John has hard conversations with cultured young leaders who want to move up and out to Austin, Portland, or Denver. "This might be an armpit," John joked with me, "but even the armpit of a supermodel is beautiful."

One Easter they decided to hold a baptism service in a local park. Easter that year fell on April 20, which is basically a state holiday in Colorado, due to its association with marijuana culture. They decided to call their baptism service "How would Jesus 4/20?" John had a theory: "He would rise from the dead and bring others with him!" About 150 people attended the service, including a number of curious onlookers. Sixteen people spontaneously decided to get baptized that day. John told me, "It was like watching fish trying to jump back in the water."

A lady named Cheryl was baptized that day. One of the many poor and broken people served by The Pearl, Cheryl suffered from a number of illnesses, including alcoholism. She recently passed away; at the hospital she had listed The Pearl Church as her next of kin.

This group of courageous ordinaries is not doing anything they think is remarkable. They battle discouragement. They work with a lot of messy people with cracked stories. Ministry is hard, but they are committed to staying well in their city and creating a new narrative in their place. In a city people think smells like armpits they are giving off the fragrance of hope.

SEEING THE CRACKS

Many times we intentionally choose not to get close to the realities of the place around us because it will be too painful. We don't want to find the real story, because we might feel obligated to do something or feel disenfranchised when our meager efforts aren't enough. Here's the beautiful and hard reality: On our own we can only make small cosmetic changes to our places. But with the gospel we can see transformation. The gospel is the mortar that fills the cracks in our places.

Most places experience the hard dynamics of advantage versus disadvantage and pride versus shame. There are strange differences between the east and west side of my city, but the socioeconomic divide between north and south sides of my city is tragic. People who have the means migrate north in my city, not south. They are looking for the better schools, proximity to good jobs, a safer place for family, and people who look a whole lot more like them. People will relocate before their kids start school so they can have better opportunities in a different school district. A friend of mine taught at a school that was infamous for teen pregnancy, drugs, and student turnover. He checked his e-mail every day hoping to get a teaching opportunity on the north side.

People often ask us, "Are you going to get your kids into the schools up north?" While my wife and I realize the educational advantage that could afford our kids, we have decided to settle for slightly less expertise in formal education in exchange for better "people education" on the south side. With two kids adopted from Ethiopia, socioeconomic, racial, and family diversity is important to us. Where we live now is not upscale; neither is it the worst place in our city. But living here we come in close contact with people who have harder stories than ours. We have people in our life who deal with the challenges of low-income housing. We regularly encounter families who look much different from ours. We have learned to value these things and talk through them with our kids. Like any parent I feel impulses to protect my kids from hard things, but we also believe we have a unique opportunity to be salt and light right here in the crazy and normal things happening in our city, to see God work through our family in school, at work, at play, in our hobbies, and in our hospitality.

CITIES ARE ALIVE

Gentrification is the word used to describe a process common to cities: attracting higher-paid residents and upscale businesses to areas that have fallen on hard times. Old homes in old neighborhoods are either renovated or razed; new, innovative housing is built on top of them. Neighborhoods can quickly turn from "the other side of the tracks" to "the hippest new hood." While this is a developer's dream and can appear to be a big win for the city, gentrification brings hard realities as well. This rebuilding drives up housing prices and often forces longtime residents to move elsewhere. The relocation of new, wealthy people into a neighborhood can cause dislocation of those who have for so long called that place home.

I'm not taking a stance on the value of gentrification, but it's something that seems inevitable in cities. I even wonder how my neighborhood will change. My neighborhood isn't old enough to be cool or new enough to be luxurious. It just is. But how will it change in ten years, after many current residents move or pass away? How will the neighborhood ecosystem change with each new resident?

No one believes they live in a perfect place, but we all long for our place to become better. The human heart beats for old, broken-down things to be pieced back together as their communities become more whole, more connected, and teeming with life again. As followers of Jesus, we aren't aiming for perfection; we are aiming for transformation. This impulse expresses our longing for the *shalom* God has woven deep into our fabric. God is on his throne; we are invited to join him in renewing things right now—to see things on earth as they are in heaven. Pursuing wholeness in our communities fulfills this commission, but it also connects us to our neighbors, followers of Jesus or not.

REDEEMING SPACES

As I walked down a sidewalk in a Rust Belt city, I spotted a large stained-glass window. We walked in to find a transformed church space. We met one of the pastors, and he explained how it used to be an infamous bar. The team from this church plant had rescued the old stained-glass window from a decommissioned Catholic church and placed it in front of their huge storefront window right next to their well-designed steampunk coffee bar. Spaces like this are popping up all over. Several churches in my city collaborated to turn an old school into a community center, park, and community garden. An urban church startup in another city moved into a warehouse in an up-and-coming arts district; they hold community gatherings for neighborhood planning in their building. Many churches have turned spaces of entertainment, business, or debauchery into spaces of worship, connection, and service to their community. Missional communities in any number of cities gather under pavilions, in art galleries, in living rooms, on back porches, and in pubs as a visible sign that God is at work everywhere. A friend of mine planted a church in California that used to meet outdoors. He is sad about the day they got "kicked into" a building.

One of the greatest ways we can let people know the Kingdom of God triumphs over the kingdom of this world is by redeeming spaces. There are spaces all around us waiting to be used as spaces for God's people to gather and scatter as salt and light. The church family I pastor bought and remodeled an old movie theater, and from time to time people come in and ask for a tour. They reminisce about the days of their feet sticking to the floors and following the rope lights down each of the aisles with buckets of overpriced popcorn. One man who had recently been baptized told me he occasionally felt guilty when he walked into our church building. He said, "I used to sneak into bad movies and make out with my girlfriend." We got a good laugh over that one.

God is in the restoration business, and he invites us to become his partners. We can partner in the process of busted-up things becoming beautiful again, making a theological statement to those around us as we do. Jesus' church cannot be limited to a building, but it can take up meaningful residence in one. God's desires are bigger than your city, but they are big enough to include the healing of your city.

QUESTIONS FOR REFLECTION AND DISCUSSION

What events or stories have shaped the narrative of your place? What cracks in your city burden you?

How can you tell an alternative story of God at work in your place?

Can you map out the characters in your place? Would others truly consider you a character in your place?

4

A ROOTED GOSPEL

"It's amazing that in a culture much more communal than ours, the early followers of Jesus were recognized as an exceptionally loving community."

PAUL SPARKS, TIM SOERENS, AND DWIGHT FRIESEN, *THE NEW PARISH*

"Better is a neighbor who is near than a brother who is far away."

PROVERBS 27:10

ONE OF MY favorite spots in my city is a view from some high bluffs. From there I can see the whole city in its whole context. One time I went there alone to do some thinking, and something unusual happened: I began to feel the dividing lines in our city like I never had before. I thought about prejudice, regional idols we bow to, and the stigmas my city is constantly trying to overcome. It ripped me apart, and I lost it. I'm not a crier, but I began to weep over our city. For all my love for Colorado Springs, somehow I had managed to neglect these realities and even contribute to them.

That was a transformative moment for me. Now I like to

take newbies to the high bluffs to talk through these issues and pray for the realities we face. To most people this spot functions as "makeout point," but for me this spot serves as a reminder that God is at work.

We only hear of Jesus weeping twice in Scripture: once over a dead friend, and once over a dying city. After the crowds laid palm branches beneath the donkey on which Jesus rode into Jerusalem, he looked over a divided city and took on its pain. He saw the issues and knew the division Jerusalem would always face.

Do you weep for your city? Maybe you'll never cry physical tears for your place, but the pain and divisions in our cities should grieve us and move us to compassion. Places mattered to Jesus, and they should matter to us.

Jesus' ministry was rooted within a very small area. He didn't travel over oceans like Paul did; Jesus chose to spend his life in an area the size of New Jersey. He was born in a disrespected place, and he grew up in one. He traveled by foot to strategic cities in Galilee to proclaim and embody the reality of the Kingdom of God at hand. You're not a failure if you don't grow up and move out to a grand place. You can live your life in a small radius and make a big impact.

WHEN WE STAY, THE GOSPEL TAKES OFF

What comes to mind when you think of Saint Patrick? Unfortunately, most people think more about green beer than they do of faithful presence. But Patrick was not only an amazing missionary who saw many hostile tribesmen come to know Jesus; he was one of the greatest church planters and movement makers of all time.[1]

As a boy Patrick was taken captive by Irish tribesmen and brought to Ireland as a slave. Eventually he escaped and returned to England, but he could not fight the call to go back to Ireland as a missionary, to proclaim the great gospel of Jesus in a place he could not forget.

Patrick was trained in ministry under a top-heavy church hierarchy that never felt right to him. Out of his love for the people of Ireland, he developed incredible missionary methods, ministering to tribes with brilliant contextualization. The gospel Patrick preached rooted itself in Irish soil; it's no wonder this rooted gospel made sense to the people, and Ireland was quickly Christianized. Patrick is now known as one of the greatest incarnational missionaries of all time.

Unlike Patrick, the apostle Paul's ministry seems to be a place-to-place journey of ministry ADD. It's easy to imagine Paul as a vagabond, gypsy traveler, barely unpacking his bags in one city before leaving again for another. Yes, he covered a lot of ground, but one of his most strategic decisions was to put down roots in Ephesus.

Ephesus at the time of Paul was a center for trade, culture, idolatry, and philosophy—a critical port and a hub for the whole region of Asia Minor. Paul spent three months boldly proclaiming the Kingdom of God in the synagogue there, but then he decided it was time to take a different approach.

> But when some became stubborn and continued
> in unbelief, speaking evil of the Way before the
> congregation, he withdrew from them and took
> the disciples with him, reasoning daily in the hall
> of Tyrannus. This continued for two years, so that
> all the residents of Asia heard the word of the Lord,
> both Jews and Greeks.   ACTS 19:9-10

Paul could have left Ephesus when some critics started "speaking evil of the Way"; he could have simply moved to his next dot on the map. But he didn't. He chose to grow roots in Ephesus in order to see the Word of the Lord grow wings and fly throughout Asia Minor. What an amazing hinge moment for the gospel!

How could your city help to spread the gospel throughout your area? A friend of mine tells me that the North American cities seeing great momentum toward gospel movements have one thing in common: people there have invested themselves for a long time, faithfully sowing the gospel and raising up leaders. These city catalysts have gradually developed trust through sustained relationships with followers of Jesus and those far from God alike. Over time that trust develops into partnership, and gradually a web of gospel champions and catalysts is created.

Staying is not only a way to live out faithfulness; it might be the most strategic thing you do for the gospel.

START AT HOME

The place you already live is the most obvious, but most overlooked, place to start ministry. The church was born to a Spirit-filled group of disciples who expected to see the gospel spread from their place to the whole world.

> But you will receive power when the Holy Spirit has come upon you, and you will be my witnesses in Jerusalem and in all Judea and Samaria, and to the end of the earth.   ACTS 1:8

When rightly applied, the gospel propels us in an outward direction. Joining the mission of God busts through our comfort zone and calls us out into nontraditional ways of loving people. We are invited to be sent ones, taking on Jesus' mission to seek and save the lost—but also taking on Jesus' incarnational posture.

In the ministry of Jesus, the work of the disciples, and the historic spread of the gospel, we see a local faith that went global. Without local witness, a region can never hear the gospel, and our world can never catch fire for Jesus. The gospel must start in our front yards. Here is a helpful incarnational mantra: Do what you can with what you've been given *where* you've been given it. Understood this way, applying the gospel in this moment to those right around you is a stewardship issue.

FINDING COLLECTIVE OVERLAP

One night my neighbors walked into my house to retrieve their kids. They found about twenty folks gathered around a couple, with hands laid on them, praying intensely for their future ministry. We were having a commissioning time for that couple at the end of a long discipleship process. This led to an awkward few minutes of collective overlap—one of those times when my friends who don't know Jesus were met by my friends who do know Jesus. But those few minutes generated great conversations with my neighbor afterward.

A key element of incarnational ministry is intentionally creating collective overlap where all those we call friends can gather—Christian and non-Christian—in one common space.

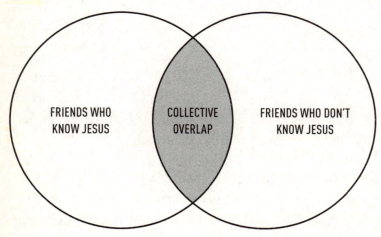

FRIENDS WHO KNOW JESUS   COLLECTIVE OVERLAP   FRIENDS WHO DON'T KNOW JESUS

I used to have no collective overlap of friends who knew Jesus and friends who didn't. I would talk about my friends on either side of this spectrum, but they would never meet one another. My friends who didn't know Jesus never got to see the beauty of Christian community; my friends who love Jesus never got to enjoy the company of non-Christians. What's worse, this partitioning of my relationships had a more insidious effect: there was a fundamental gap in my relationships— on one side, Christian friends; on the other side, outreach projects. Something about this never felt right to me.

Finding collective overlap not only addressed the primary problems of an insular Christian community and a lack of exposure to the gospel among my non-Christian friends; it helped me to close the gap between outreach and relationship. My non-Christian friends were no longer projects; they were friends. The gospel became not something I was selling, but something I was living and weaving into every aspect of relationships.

Intentionally creating collective overlap for people who do know Jesus and those who don't is a risk, but it's surprisingly simple: our front yards, living rooms, and social gatherings are great, natural spaces for collective overlap to occur. Most folks I meet already have some collective overlap, but they have never intentionally developed it.

WHEN I GET THAT FEELING I WANT CONTEXTUAL HEALING

Loving our place and the people who reside there will naturally lead us to contextualize our ministry methods. Our focus will shift from practicing strategy on people to feeling the texture of their souls and stories.[2] When we draw near to people we get the privilege of seeing their hurt and joy up close.

One of the central tasks of the missionary is to exegete the culture of our place and to translate the gospel into that culture. Exegesis and translation both take time. Place-based people learn to take the role of spiritual investigators, scouring their community for clues of how and why it functions. As the authors of *The New Parish* observe, "The gospel becomes so much more tangible and compelling when the local church is actually part of the community, connected to the struggles of the people and even the land itself."[3] In other words, God's people become translators of the Good News when we are rooted in relationships and places.

In order to translate we must apply practical wisdom to speaking in the heart language and rhythms the people understand. In every place there are assumptions that could be completely wrong. "These people don't want to engage in relationships." "They aren't interested in Jesus." "That neighbor is creepy." "They don't talk to us because they don't like us." "Our neighbors are closed off to the world." "My coworker thinks she's better than me" "This kind of thing would never work in this part of town." We are quite skilled at judging people based on assumptions that often aren't true.

Assumptions destroy neighborhoods and relationships. They also destroy our gospel influence. Disconnection squelches our relationships and keeps us from learning to love others. To burst the bubble of surface-level relationships, we need to push through assumptions about people. God gives us compassion for others, but compassion is fueled through relationship. How can we love those we don't know?

Faithful presence cannot be sustained through grit and conviction alone. Jon Tyson says, "The only thing that can sustain incarnational ministry is love. Legalism, moralism, obligation, vision or energy will not be able to sustain it."[4] Whether we start with love for a people or love for a place, we must all learn to see people and love them as Jesus does.

No matter how you are wired, you can learn to engage with the people in your place with the love of Jesus. Digging deep with people in your place isn't about being an introvert or an extrovert; it's about being a child of God. We can unleash his love on others in extraordinary and ordinary ways. There's no perfect strategy to start loving your place and its people, but at some point we all must learn to join the journey.

CHANGE THE PARADIGM, CHANGE THE NEIGHBORHOOD

Leaders of a church plant in Denver, one of America's most transient cities, were told by well-meaning church leaders in various cities not to waste their time with anything resembling church membership, because the urban core they were trying to reach simply wouldn't commit to anything. After comparing this advice to the foundation of covenant running through the veins of Scripture, however, they realized they couldn't agree. Scripture is chock full of covenant commitments between God and his people, and they were going to lean into that notion of covenant. They simply couldn't deny what they knew was deep in the heart of God.

So my friends launched the Roots Campaign. They challenged young, urban, cultured, outdoor-loving Jesus-followers to make a long-term commitment to the Five Points neighborhood in Denver. In a place people migrate to largely to consume the culture and the mountains, the Roots Campaign challenged people not simply to serve the city but to put down roots there. Some people resisted, and it led to great conversations. But many decided to buy homes in Five Points and commit to one day raising kids there. Many made a sacrificial commitment to regularly give to the mission of the church.

This church has become a stable and visible presence in that neighborhood. When I pulled up to attend their service, I would have thought it was the porch spilling out from a coffee shop or brewery. People were laughing and making a scene. It was electric. The church has hosted neighborhood gatherings in their warehouse-turned-worship-and-community-space. Couples have chosen to hold their weddings in this space. Although it has not been easy for this church, they had the guts to change a paradigm—about how people live in a city, and about what churches can expect of their members—and God is using them to change Five Points.

There will always be popular advice that leads us away from commitment; often that advice pulls us away from the foundations of Scripture. I am thankful my friends ignored the advice to resist commitment. I think the city of Denver is glad too.

QUESTIONS FOR REFLECTION AND DISCUSSION

What are some specific things you can do to develop collective overlap between friends who know Jesus and friends who do not?

In what ways could your city or neighborhood be a strategic hub for the gospel?

What are some ordinary ways you can start the practice of faithfully loving those around you?

5

THE GLORY OF THE MUNDANE

"We are not redeemed from the mundane. We are redeemed from the slavery of thinking our mundane life is not enough."

MATTHEW REDMOND, *THE GOD OF THE MUNDANE*

"Ecstasy doesn't last. But it can cut a channel for something lasting."

E. F. FORSTER

"Ambition tempts us to forsake the mundane for the sake of unlimited growth—or, at least, new opportunities. We are so easily unimpressed by the ordinary."

JONATHAN WILSON-HARTGROVE, *THE WISDOM OF STABILITY*

KATIE WAS A missions-minded follower of Jesus. Everyone around her knew she was willing to go anywhere God told her. One night some friends were gathered, and she said she had something to share with us: she and two friends were going to do missions—right here in Colorado Springs. These single ladies had decided to relocate to a local, under-resourced trailer park. They saw massive needs in this area, and they were intentionally moving there. They had decided to pit the gospel against the American Dream and see which came out on top.

"Honestly," Katie tells me, "before the year we moved into the trailer, I would have told you with a fair amount of confidence that 'going' for me was going to mean Southeast Asia or South America or anywhere overseas. I had no desire to stay in America, a place I find frustrating on many levels.

"I remember very clearly the day God told me otherwise, in his own strange way. Frankly, I was unhappy about it for a while. After that came a slew of hints—books, articles, random conversations—about moving into a low-income neighborhood. When my lease was almost up the following summer, I finally said that great word of surrender: 'Uncle!'"

The way God brought these three women together is its own story, but the end result was this: three girls in their twenties, preparing to move into a low-income neighborhood, somewhere in Colorado Springs, with little idea how their mission would unfold. "We looked at rough neighborhoods and sketchy apartment complexes, glanced at crime rates, and tried to calm our parents and friends. When we finally took a walk through a mobile home park I had stumbled upon by accident, we all three knew it was home. We moved in that August. We had not been there twenty-four hours before kids just started coming to our home."

Katie and her friends moved to the trailer park not knowing how long they would stay. They certainly didn't imagine the ministry they would encounter there for the next seven years. "In reality, the mobile home park was just a few miles from the house I had been living in, but it felt like a world away. There were some major adjustments to smells and mold and infestations of ants and mice, and neighborhood rhythms we weren't quite used to. So many things shifted inside and around us. *Want* and *need* took on nuanced meanings. Our own prejudices and assumptions were confronted constantly. Our rhythm of time and sense of space was different.

"To truly be present there, we had to recognize that we didn't 'own' our lives in the way we thought we did. My roommates in particular blew my mind with their sacrifice of time and energy and comfort. My own learning curve was slower. Hours of play and after-school snacks, rides to school and to appointments, cheering at sporting events and concerts, our Thursday community night, mealtimes shared with neighbors, knocks on the door at random. Life at the trailer was different and often hard, but so, so beautiful."

Katie and her friends were still in Colorado Springs, but their lives were focused on a part of the city they hadn't engaged before. "That had bigger implications than we expected. For a long time, we were awkwardly switching back and forth between two worlds as we moved in and out of our work, church, and home lives. The strangest thing may have been the tension in knowing that while so many things were changing for us, they had not changed at all for our friends outside the park. Even though we didn't leave the city or change jobs or churches or back out of small groups, our community changed drastically. Some of our friends struggled to relate to what we were doing, and so they grew distant and in some cases faded away entirely. Others came alongside us in very real ways, pouring themselves into our neighbors right along with us, and out of that grew a whole new level of community—family, really. Multiple weddings in those years included those of us involved daily or weekly at the trailer, and a gaggle of kids tearing it up on the dance floor."

To this day, Katie will tell you that her season in the trailer is "maybe the best season of my life. People have often praised us for what we were doing there, but we have always felt incredibly humbled by the fact that all we really did was move in and choose to be present. God did everything else. So amazingly simple. Sometimes I want to shout from church rooftops that something beautiful is waiting if we will only enter into the marginalized corners of the places we already call home."

What an incredibly simple example of being faithfully present. Perhaps the most convicting thing I experienced through the example of Katie and her friends was how their seemingly mundane ministry became anything but mundane.

FROM DISLOCATION TO RELOCATION

We have gotten sucked into the idea that God works in amazing people, places, and situations, but is silent in the ordinary spaces. Would you be okay if God let you have a ministry of relative obscurity? What if no one ever told others about how you were living out the gospel, but you were being obedient? This is challenging. I struggle through wanting something bigger, better, newer—more notable, remarkable, and radical than the long journey of simple faithfulness. Isn't there a better gimmick or an easier path?

Most of us would say we want to impact the ends of the earth, but if we're honest, we will admit that we have not left much of a mark on the Jerusalem right around us. Our eyes are busy scanning the horizon instead of praying for where God has placed us.

The lie about rooted ministry is that it's easy and boring. In reality it's exhilarating and challenging. Yes, there are mundane moments, and we must embrace them. But there are also moments of deep excitement, and breakthroughs that rarely happen on short-term trips.

One way we need to recalibrate our sense of mission is from *dislocation* to *relocation*. Dislocation is painful. Ever experienced a dislocated finger or shoulder? It may take us out of a neighborhood, community, or city we are familiar with to a place where we have no relationships. It can generate anxiety in us, which is perhaps why so few people become cross-cultural missionaries. But when it is accompanied by an aversion to the mundane, dislocation can generate a sense of adventure. You might feel an ambiguous longing in the home, relationships, and places you currently reside in; dislocation can be tempting in such a situation: "Anywhere," the Replacements once sang, "is better than here."

Abraham trusted God enough to be *dislocated from* a place of family heritage and *relocated to* an unknown place. That's a key distinction: God doesn't remove us; he places us. There is no missional dislocation, only missional relocation—even, as in Katie's example, relocation to where you already are. Maybe God has placed you in your neighborhood and you desire to be somewhere else; you may need to ask God not to dislocate you but to relocate you—to begin your ministry where you are, or to direct you to a particular place where you can locate yourself for the long term. The journey toward faithful presence can lead us from dislocation to relocation to location. But wherever we land, God beckons us to become faithfully present to our place.

THE IMPACT OF LONGEVITY

A friend and I were talking about the impact of churches over dinner one night. He said, "I'm convinced that if Christian leaders can just find ways to stay, we can see amazing things happen. Our biggest task is to keep doing ministry and not leave." I'm not promising success or minimizing the challenges of ministry, but we rarely take the impact of longevity into account. Effectiveness almost always grows over time while rooted in a place. There is a direct correlation between how long we are in a place faithfully living like Jesus and the impact we will have on people.

It is likely that ministry effectiveness increases with more time in fewer places, not fewer time in more places. Longevity, or lack thereof, has created one of the greatest paradoxes in ministry. Some studies over the years reference somewhere around four years as an average pastoral stint in one place. Many pastoral mentors in my life have shared with me that the first five years in a place had been their most challenging time of fighting for credibility and lacking impact. I believe many Christian leaders leave before they have seen much impact; some of them leave right before they have experienced impact. We expect a great impact right away, and when we don't experience that, we begin to assume things:

"I'm not a good fit for this community." "I'm not effective here." "I need to find a different vocation." "The people here aren't accepting me like they would somewhere else." There are any number of things Satan whispers to us.

One of the biggest golden calves we bow to as Western Christians is the future. We learn to look past the present, but our obsession with the future renders us ineffective and disembodied. We daydream as we wonder, "Where will God take me next? What will I do? When will I get a job in that field? What group will recognize the influence I can bring?" Our call as missionaries, however, supersedes our careers and dreams. If we are distracted by an upward career path, we will likely find ourselves disconnected from our place and the people around us.

Who pays for this preoccupation with our next assignment? Our neighbors, friends, and family—the ones right in front of our faces. There are people who will miss the opportunity to see the Kingdom of God embodied and proclaimed if we are distracted by these daydreams.

It's easy to believe the fantasy that life will be easier, smoother, and have fewer issues in the next place, but discontentment has no problem traveling with you wherever you go. Ministry always seems easier "over there." In *The Pastor,* Eugene Peterson admits to believing the same thing. "I was told about churches that were looking for a pastor. From a distance they looked pretty good. From their self-descriptions they were obviously a lot more promising than the lethargic congregation I was leading."[1]

Maybe you feel like throwing in the towel right now. Maybe you haven't told your spouse or boss, but you're looking elsewhere. You have an eye on the next place, and you're convincing yourself why you'd be more effective there. You have your eye on the effectiveness of other groups or churches, and you're convincing yourself to close up shop. Perhaps you are in process of calling it quits on a church startup, and you are convinced the only choice is to leave town. Perhaps your group, ministry, or church is in turmoil from bad leadership decisions, and you are convinced exiting now is your only choice. Maybe. But maybe moments like this are exactly when you need to stay in your place and make an impact. Maybe you need to exit full-time ministry and get a "normal" job while you focus on growing roots. Maybe you need to take a vacation, get some rest, prayer-walk your city, and ask God to help you fall in love with it again. Maybe the pay cut won't devastate your family; maybe the decisions you need to make aren't as earth-shattering as you think. Maybe it's time to dig your heels in. When you get the urge to move on to the next ministry, maybe you need to lean into God even more. Maybe you need your neighbors and the friendships you've cultivated right around you more than you think.

There was a time when my friends were experiencing victory in their lives, and I seemed to be experiencing a string of hard defeats. While my friends were experiencing much influence and God was providing in excess for their families, I seemed to be hitting constant walls, and people in every corner of my life wanted more from me than I could give. Finances were hard, and I was struggling to support my ministry habit. I wondered if I was being disobedient, if I had heard God wrong, or if I simply wasn't gifted enough to thrive in life and ministry. Discouragement is hard. Pressure to bring in the next paycheck is real. I know; I've been there many times. Discouragement is not a sign of being in the wrong place; it's a sign of being human. When you experience lows it does not mean you're not gifted and called. Your battle scars might be open wounds right now, but with time they can become stories of God's healing work.

It takes a long time to sink roots in the ground, but just a few seconds to cut down a tree. Sometimes we transplant too quickly. Sometimes staying isn't just the best thing for our ministry, it's the best thing for us.

A MIRACLE BLOOMING IN OUR 'HOOD

There is one woman who has required continual energy from my wife and me. Many times we've been discouraged, wondering if we have had any impact on her life. I will refer to this woman as Karen. In the last four years, in addition to losing her marriage, Karen has experienced three significant deaths in her life, struggled through bouts of mental illness and alcohol-related incidents. Every month she seems to experience a different form of heartbreak. There always seems to be something painful going on in her life. My wife has listened to Karen talk for long hours, giving counsel where it was wanted. We have taken care of her daughter. She has joined us nearly every Friday for coffee on the corner and at every dinner party we've thrown. She has just simply been around, soaking in relationship with our family and our band of Jesus-loving friends. We have hitchhiked with her down the road of pain she has been living. It's been exhausting and fulfilling.

One day she showed up at our church service unannounced. For several weeks she absorbed a collective glimpse of what she had experienced in our living room, at Free Coffee Friday, and in dinner parties. Tears were streaming down her face every time she sat in a church service. Something clicked. After about three years of struggling through life with Karen, she crawled in the passenger seat, tossed Jesus the keys, and let him drive. I got the great honor of baptizing her just a few weeks back. As our congregation heard her retelling her journey toward Jesus, life paused for a moment. I recounted many of those times we had felt hopeless in loving her. While we continued to love her as she was, we never imagined a day when we would celebrate this precious sacrament together. If every cup of coffee we've served and every time we've prepared food for a dinner party was to experience this part of Karen's journey, it was worth it.

We ate pizza that day and celebrated what God had done in Karen. We spoke words of destiny over her that trump the words of death she often believes. I can't promise Karen that her life will get easier. I can't promise you that faithful presence will lead to conversions and baptisms. I can promise you that faithful presence in the name of Jesus will eventually get noticed. When Jesus' church lives and moves with the grace and gutsy-ness Jesus calls us to, it makes a scene for God's Kingdom.

DON'T TRY TO CHANGE THE WORLD

The Bible has a list of stories of people who wanted to do anything but what was right in front of their faces. Moses didn't want to face Pharaoh. Joseph was dubious about taking Mary as his wife. I can bet Judah wasn't excited about living well in Babylon. Obedience is rarely easy, and faithfulness isn't glorious. Would you line up on opening weekend to watch a movie about a single mom in a small Midwestern town who loved her kids well while working two jobs and faithfully serving a few people around her in the name of Jesus? That's not the next box office hit, but that could be a life of legacy. It's not glorious, but it brings glory to God.

God has given us only so much energy. This realization should lead us to careful boundaries and stewardship, but it can also lead us to an obsession with efficiency: we want every time we serve people to have a tangible impact, to demonstrate that we are "useful" for God. There isn't a scorecard for faithfully abiding in places and relationships. We long to experience the beauty of spiritual banquets in the time it takes to serve up a Happy Meal. Something just doesn't add up.

I have been on the journey of recalibrating my vision from immediate impact to longevity. There is nothing sexy about this shift. It takes constant commitment to remembering to keep faithfulness as the metric. It's more about covenant than emotions, more about obedience than motion, more about my life being affected than affecting those around me. Ministering with Jesus is a descent into humility, not an ascent into influence.

Our task is not to have a massive impact. We want to change the world, but our true task is to be faithfully present long enough for Jesus to change the world through us. Jesus alone has the power to change hearts. We move into neighborhoods, inhabit cities, react with grace, occupy cubicles, celebrate those around us, grieve for the cracks in our world, all the while learning to find beauty in the mundane.

As a boy I knew Cal Ripken as an All-Star player for the Baltimore Orioles. Now I see him as a hero with a unique story we can all learn from. Cal had incredible feats on the field: named rookie of the year, twice awarded the Gold Glove, an All-Star nineteen times, with 431 home runs in the major leagues. He is now in the Baseball Hall of Fame. But more than anything, the mark Cal leaves on baseball is his consistency. No player in baseball kept showing up like Cal did. Many people refer to the moment he broke Lou Gehrig's streak for the most consecutive games played, with 2,132, as the "most memorable moment in baseball history." I remember watching him take a lap around Camden Yards and touching hands of the fans who had watched him mature for twenty-one years in the same city, on the same team.

Most people don't know Cal Ripken grew up Aberdeen, Maryland, a town of about fifteen thousand. After retiring from professional baseball, Cal bought and relocated a minor league baseball team there!

One picture burned into my memory had a fan holding up a sign with the acrostic, "C.A.L. Class. Ability. Longevity." Longevity is underrated in our world today. Cal Ripken left a legacy in baseball. In a time where players move from team to team chasing money and fame, this hometown Maryland boy stayed through the good and the bad.

What if Christians sought to become the Cal Ripkens of their cities? What if, instead of celebrating admittedly gifted speakers, writers, and leaders, we celebrated (and emulated) people like Katie and her friends, people embodying the faithfulness of longevity?

Faithful presence has fewer dividends in the moment. It is a slow burn, but a burn that can make the name of Jesus famous in alleys, pubs, trailer parks, schools, front yards, and third places.

QUESTIONS FOR REFLECTION AND DISCUSSION

Which "mundane" areas are hardest for you to serve others in?

What are some steps you can take to move from dislocation from your place and relationships to relocation in them?

How have you experienced the favor of longevity among people?

6

THE RISK OF WINGS

"The church can be the alternative and the antidote to the excarnational impulses in society today."

MICHAEL FROST, *INCARNATE*

"The development of meaningful relationships where every member carries a significant sense of belonging is central to what it means to be the Church."

RANDY FRAZEE, *THE CONNECTING CHURCH*

My name is Alan, and I have a problem with wanderlust. There, I said it. I have always wanted to travel to every space on earth and experience every culture I possibly can. I was blessed to grow up in a family where travel and cross-cultural experiences were a higher value than possessions. I had traveled to more countries by the age of fifteen than most people experience their whole lives. I have always had the habit of leafing through travel magazines and planning my next expeditions. It is not hard for me to summon the energy to dream up road trips, camping excursions, and other adventures.

I took full advantage of my time in Antarctica. I took the cannonball into a hole in the ice called the Polar Plunge, joined an international bowling team, ran a marathon, and snowboarded down a volcano. After my season of work there I decided to spend a few months in New Zealand, where a friend and I met strangers at hostels, campsites, and climbing areas, and banded together with newfound friends to go on some of the best adventures of my life.

The local Kiwis said they were jealous of us. Most of them were busy with work and family in their small towns, and we had no responsibility. But eventually the portable adventure life began to wear us down, and I envied the simple lives the local Kiwis had made. I was jealous of their roots; they were jealous of my wings.

Wanderlust is a kind of lust: built on a false reality, pursuing pleasure without commitment. Lust takes what it wants, what makes it feel good, and throws out anything else. It's always easier to lust after other places than to face the hard realities of our own place. Wanderlust is going to a beach town on vacation and thinking the weather is always perfect and locals just hang out at the beach every day. We idealize the lives of those living in our dream place while we dread returning to the issues and realities that await us back home. The term *wander* is far more welcome than the word *lust* in our culture. But lust is what we're talking about: "Do you know what lust is? Lust is when you actively force your own priority on someone else."[1]

Beware of the temptation to pass by the realities and think the grass is greener on the other side—the more beautiful, more affluent, safer side. Wings are not sinful, but neither are they a remedy for the risk of roots. Taking flight to a new place does not remove your problems; it simply causes you to face new ones.

SPIRITUAL HOMELESSNESS

Why are wings so appealing? There are several reasons.

Wings offer an escape from current realities. The place we are in represents the realities of our lives. Many of them are hard realities of money, strained relationships, jobs, stress, meaninglessness, and lack of leisure. Most of us have had some amazing moments on our winged journeys away from home. Heading off to college, going on global mission trips, taking vacations on other continents, and exploring new cultures are all thrilling things. But sometimes in the process of growing wings we can put our hope in a new horizon or a past season instead of putting our hope in Jesus.

Wings help us realize our potential. Perhaps the narrative of your place involves someone who escaped to pursue better education, a more fulfilling career, and more money. Some people grow up in places where you are told, "Get out or get sucked in." Wings offer new opportunities to use our gifts fully, to change the world, and to experience things we often can't experience at home. Nevertheless, our ultimate potential is found not in some other place but in the hope of Jesus.

Wings can scratch the itch for adventure. For some, home represents the boredom of routine. We love seeing amazement in others when we tell our travel stories and show them the pictures on our mantel. To this day I still get a happy feeling when I walk into airports remembering all the great trips my family took when I was growing up. I remember all the risks I took crossing continents and leaning into new potential. This happy feeling, the pride of experience, can be addicting, so that we crave more and more adventure and neglect our routine responsibilities that represent most of our time on this earth. Wings make for a great experience, but they easily turn into terrible idols.

STOP PAYING RENT

We are constantly tempted to lift our eyes from our communities and the people right around us to find the next place "God will call us." The longing for a perfectly placed call of God has led many Christians into a head-on collision with transience. Sociologist Peter Berger says, "Modern man has suffered from a deepening condition of 'homelessness'. The result of the migratory character of his experience of society and of self has been called a metaphysical loss of home."[2] Michael Frost refers to this loss of home as "psycho-spiritual homelessness."[3] I call it paying spiritual rent. We need to learn to pay spiritual mortgages right where we're at.

The irony of routine is that while we often can't wait to escape it, without it we often lose our purpose and self-destruct. We look forward to recovering from the crazy "breaks" we take. We need a vacation from vacation. December is probably the most haphazard, frenetic thirty-one days of the year; in January our desire for routine resettles us. We have undersold the value of routine that can keep us grounded to God's desires.

Something happens to us when we start paying a mortgage: We take better care of our home, our yard, our relationships when we know we are staying. We become more present. Renters don't have to fix the water heater when it goes, but they also rarely cultivate long-lasting relationships in a place. Just as a house we have invested in gains equity the more payments we make, we gain equity in our relationships over time. There is a scary risk in making long-term investments, in people and a place, but there is also a grounding and settling that occurs. Some would call it responsibility; some might call it stewardship.

In their book *The Faith of Leap* Michael Frost and Alan Hirsch observe that the Western church is "suffering from a sense of suburban homelessness, never at home in its local neighborhood."[4] They are describing the essence of displacement: we have a place, but we are somehow removed from it. We are *dis*placed. When I invite people to join us in serving our neighborhood, I explain who the people around us are and give specific instructions of what we are hoping to accomplish. I try to prepare them for how they can partner with what God is already doing here. We have worked hard for credibility in our neighborhood, and sometimes I legitimately fear that others from outside our context will leave a stain that will hurt our credibility. My neighbors are a curiosity to outsiders, but to me they are my neighbors. Long after our guests leave our neighborhood, we will still be praying for our neighbors and aiming to build deeper relationship with them.

RETHINKING MISSION TRIPS

The idea of long-term commitments applies not only to our particular place. Our global missions efforts can sometimes drift into a form of conquering. We put a pin on a map and say, "Been there. Done that. Got the T-shirt." While there is certainly nothing wrong with mission trips, we can accidentally slip into "missions tourism" attending the "missions vacation" of our choice. Emily Wierenga, author of *Atlas Girl*, reflects about "religious tourism."

> On these trips we view another part of the world and how they live, and we have our hearts moved for the things that move God. These trips usually help us, but not necessarily them.
>
> And that's okay as long as we don't inflict harm in the process; so long as we don't go there to use the locals. So long as we don't go there with the wrong motive or impression: to erase some white guilt or to do an act of service that will somehow "fix" the world. Not only do these attitudes shame, versus dignify, the national, but they also prevent us from understanding the humility of our situation or the majesty of God.

Wierenga suggests we ask the question, "Will your church or organization continue to follow up with the people you've met with the intention of developing a long-term relationship?"[5]

Perhaps your church, missional community, or group of

friends needs to move from one-off short-term mission trips to long-term partnership with a particular group of people. Perhaps your church or group needs to nestle into a partnership with a large global ministry that is well-versed in the needs and realities on the ground. Perhaps you can reconsider who goes as a representative of your group. What if groups of Christians pooled money together to send healthcare professionals, teachers, or small business owners to places where locals have deemed those needs as paramount? I'm not proposing we stop going on mission trips, but that we consider sending small, better-resourced teams of folks with an eye toward long-term development, healthcare, education, and microfinancing. We can go as learners and investigators, rather than as answer people. We must remember what is global to us is local to others. Just like my neighbors, the people we visit on our mission trips will still live in their communities once we have flown home. For good or for ill they will have to manage what we did.

The gospel propels us outward, but perhaps we've interpreted *outward* simply to mean long-distance. You're not a second-class Christian if you never cross an ocean or leave your town for a mission trip. The goal of mission trips is to join God's mission; joining God's mission does not necessarily require a trip. Living in the outward direction is a posture, not a destination. The gospel propels us away from ourselves, our desires, and our security. When the decision to stay in a place is understood missionally, the impact of faithful presence usually increases. Maybe the decision to skip the next mission trip and invest locally is the gutsy call you need to make.

I'm not saying mission trips are inherently harmful or consumeristic. Jesus was clear we are to "make disciples of all nations" (Matthew 28:19). But we have to be careful not to view national or global mission trips—collecting experiences in exotic places—as the *only* expression of missions. Today the opportunities for reaching the nations can happen by going *or* by staying. Decades of globalization have brought the world to us. Many Christians have "a heart for the nations," buy fair-trade products, wear TOMS shoes, sponsor a child, and pray for unreached people groups. But many of those same Christians can't tell you the names of their neighbors. We have accidentally depersonalized missions by imagining villages halfway across the world instead of our next-door neighbors. Don't use global engagement as an excuse for local disengagement.

We need to continue praying for, serving, and traveling to other nations to show and tell of the life-transforming story of Jesus. Just be careful of ministry wanderlust leading you to miss people right under your nose. We need to use the resources God has given us to help those close and those far away.

I am an advocate of churches and families making long-term commitments to serve in a particular place. Our church has entered a long-term partnership with two church plants in Ecuador through a larger organization, and I am looking forward to staying in that partnership for many years to come. My wife and I anticipate taking our kids on trips to Ecuador and watching them gain relationships with the churches in that region, as well as the churches they will plant. Hopefully five, ten, fifteen years down the line, we will understand and serve the needs of our friends in Ecuador better than we can today.

TRADING INCARNATION FOR MISSION

I will never forget a mission trip I took to Mexico when I was sixteen. I felt a boldness to proclaim the gospel through my broken Spanish. I loved the adrenaline rush of gospel boldness, but I never talked to any of those people again.

I find myself longing for the boldness of being on a foreign mission trip with the credibility and familiarity of living next door. That is a gospel of both mission and incarnation.

All Christians are to be "sent ones," joining God in his renewing work. Followers of Jesus are to be saint-equippers; churches are to be equipping and deployment centers. There are few things more fulfilling than laying hands on a group of people who know they have been called into God's mission and accept the call—whether it's to move across town or across the world. When we send people, we are actually just affirming a sending God doing *his* sending work in and through them. Sending your best leaders with true joy is one of the hardest things we can do, but it's one of the most fruitful. My heart breaks when I hear friends share how they were kicked to the curb by their church leadership when they shared their sense of call to go somewhere else. In our church we consider it an honor to bring church planters up on our stage during a weekend service, affirm God's work in their lives, and invite some of our best people to go with them. I am excited to hear rumblings of churches all over the world doing this! This is good news to our people and to the ones they will reach with the gospel.

While the North American church is starting to catch on to the missional side of "going well," we are largely devoid of the incarnational side of "staying well." There's something exciting about traversing the world and sending other leaders to do so. Staying does not conjure the same emotions or fund-raising efforts. Committing to stay in one place and work for its good might be the most countercultural and transformative thing we can do. We must be careful to not be all mission, no incarnation.

Jesus was sent to earth by his Father to accomplish redemptive work as *the* great missionary, but he did this by means of incarnation. Jesus put on flesh and lived among the dirty and sweaty mess of humanity. We must be careful to not take on the mission of Jesus without also taking on his incarnational approach. Mission devoid of incarnation leads to a posture of conquest. Incarnation without mission leads to a posture of acceptance where we lose the desire to let Jesus spill out of us. Both are dangers.

The Great Commission, commonly translated as "go and make disciples" (NIV), can more accurately be translated as "as you are going, make disciples." We have opportunities to make disciples as we weave through our days—in the coffee shop, on the bleachers at our kids' soccer practice, during an awkward conversation with a coworker, on our driveway talking with our neighbor. Staying attuned to God's love for others around us launches us into disciple-making. We can look up from answering e-mails and choose to join the water cooler conversation. We can pray for the strangers around us at the café. We can schedule the dinner we have been talking about with the neighbors for the last year. We can deliver food or offer childcare to the struggling family we invited to "give us a holler if you need anything." We can set up a time to meet with that friend who is curious about Jesus. Throughout our daily conversations, meals, activities, and play, every moment is an opportunity to embody Jesus to those around us.

The most formidable "mission trips" I ever attended were the closest to home. Twice I had the opportunity to go to "the other side of the tracks," the place folks in my own town were scared of, and invest a week of my life in a neighborhood. I might as well have crossed an ocean. Just miles away from the utopia of our downtown area, voted several times as the nicest place to live in our country, was a complex set of issues and a lot of pain. These neighborhoods were much different culturally and racially from mine. People there worried about different things than I did. I would lie awake at night hearing sounds I wasn't used to. I walked streets I had never walked and finally understood the other side of our city—not just the part I knew and was proud of.

In all honesty, these two trips rocked me to the core and changed my view of my town and of mission. I realized I didn't have to drive states away or hop on a plane to partner with the Father. In the year that followed I was able to tutor kids from those neighborhoods, lead summer camps, and help them shop for their parents' Christmas gifts.

This type of immersive local mission is becoming more popular. In a time where money can be scarce and people in North America are losing interest in attending a church, maybe we should take the risk of bringing the church to our own place. My friend built a relationship with some homeless men living under a bridge. After he accepted an invitation to experience a few days and nights living as they lived, he cannot think about our city the same.

From military to missions organizations, my city is a trampoline to the world. I have observed over time there are people floating around my city, their lives stuck in limbo. For whatever reason they weren't able to launch across the world, but they feel called to be missionaries. When I meet these folks, I invite them into our ten-month training process for everyday missionaries. The beauty is always in the moment when they say, "I am realizing I can be a missionary right here in this city. I don't *have* to go overseas, although some-day I might *get* to go overseas." Bingo! As we equip people for mission, local training can function as both a strategy to reach your place for Jesus and a training ground for the future. If God takes someone across the world later, then you've equipped a missionary who's both local and global.

THE SNEAKY LIE OF DESTINATION CITIES

Like most afternoons in Southern California, it was a beautiful one. My wife and I were reuniting with a friend who had moved out to Los Angeles to chase her acting dream. Most of the afternoon we let her talk and lick her wounds. She felt let down. The image of L.A. our culture has projected hadn't matched up to her experience. She was struggling to make ends meet with people she barely knew and rent she could barely pay. Our friend needed to be reminded that God loved her, we loved her, and our city—her home—was still a good place to live. She moved back sixty days later.

The reality about destination cities is they aren't actually lying to us; they give us an excuse to lie to ourselves. There are even destination cities for Christian leaders. They usually offer opportunity for a bigger platform, or they seem post-Christian enough to offer a hefty ministry challenge. Both are rooted in discontentment and can be an equal farce.

THE DANGER OF TAKING A CITY

Western Christians love conquest and challenge. We love leading the charge and getting credit. Plus, there is a start and an end to conquering something or someone. It's a task we can focus on and check off a list.

The posture of conquest, however, can lead to colonization. This was often the case in the early days of overseas missions. In addition to sharing the gospel, European missionaries would bring their culturally conditioned ways of organizing the churches with them. It was sophisticated and European and didn't match non-Western settings and lifestyles. These well-intentioned missionaries asked non-Western people to adapt to Western ways of life, language, and ministry. They lumped it all together and called it the gospel.

We can unknowingly make the same mistake. Incarnational ministry is rooted in sacrificial love. We love others into relationship with Jesus. But spiritual conquest and colonization liken people to projects we must accomplish, and these vulnerabilities are aggravated by a short-term, unrooted posture toward a place. If we are relationally investing in people today but gone tomorrow, we can leave people feeling abandoned and devalued.

A friend told me a striking story about the battle between transience and faithful presence. He works among the homeless in our city. Once or twice a year, he tells me, a large group from a church would arrive in a local park, a gathering place for homeless people. Wearing matching church T-shirts, they would serve a meal to the homeless folks in the park. A few hours later, they would pack up, not returning until the next year. My friend wondered why this church wouldn't be interested in weekly or monthly partnership with him and his ministry, who had a stable presence among the homeless multiple times a week and were in deep friendships with these people. But no contact from them until the next year, for another meal, decked out in their matching T-shirts.

Perhaps the greatest disadvantage of wings with no roots is a lack of personal credibility. This will lead to a lack of credibility for the gospel you proclaim and seek to embody.

Incarnation seeks to live out the gospel in rhythms and language people can understand. It's not about driving in and sharing the gospel as an outsider, but about embodying the gospel in the ordinary moments and spaces of life. You don't have to live next to the church building to demonstrate faithful presence. Even if you live several neighborhoods away from where your church gathers, you can be the aroma of Christ to the people in proximity to you.

Don't be fooled; growing wings is an appealing idea, but it is a massive risk. For some with a missionary mind-set it's a calculated risk and worth taking, but many who succumb to flight fantasies are left weary, disconnected, and unfulfilled. It's time for us to count the cost of wings versus roots; when we do, the inherent value of roots, to ourselves and our neighbors, becomes clear.

QUESTIONS FOR REFLECTION AND DISCUSSION

What changes do you need to make to shift from paying spiritual rent to the community investment mentality of paying a spiritual mortgage?

How can your family, church, or organization rethink global missions for more sustainability?

In which areas of your life does your posture toward nonbelievers need to change to become more incarnational?

7

THE RISK OF ROOTS

"The challenge we face as followers of the Incarnate one is to move from the posture of tourist, to the posture of pilgrims."

LEONARD HJALMARSON, *INTRODUCTION TO A THEOLOGY OF PLACE*

"To be rooted is perhaps the most important and least recognized need of the human soul."

SIMONE WEIL, *THE NEED FOR ROOTS*

"IF THIS CHURCH plant doesn't make it, are you going to stay?" Most church planters are caught off guard when I ask them this. I love sitting down over coffee and hearing the faith stories that have led people to start new churches in my city. I honestly believe we need to be tripping over each other, birthing new churches in every neighborhood. I want church planters to know I love them and honor the risks they have taken—but I also love my city and have seen the damage of churches and leaders coming and going. I want to know if we're going to be doing ministry together for several years.

One church planter in our city was going door to door telling people about his church, which would be gathering in the school down the street. A woman answered her door, and he quickly assured her he wasn't selling anything, and then excitedly began to share his vision with her. But she stopped him. "I've gotten door hangers before, and I've even talked to others like you, telling me about their new church meeting in that same school. None of them are still here. You are just one more church who won't be here in a few years."

My friend was shocked. He had just gotten a free education on the value of staying. Not only had the woman at the door felt devalued by past churches she had been invited to, she had lost trust that *the church* cared about her.

A few days after we moved into our neighborhood, our family began to venture out and explore a bit. I was outside, looking over our serious landscaping predicament, when a woman across the street came over to me. "Welcome to the neighborhood," she said. "The people who used to live here were pretty well loved. Good luck living up to their reputation."

I didn't know what to think. I was both taken aback and challenged. There was a standard, a high expectation for us to live well here. A neighbor who doesn't share our faith convictions was reminding us to lean in and stay well.

These encounters show us the importance of longevity and the dangers of transience. People are skeptical of things that are here today and gone tomorrow. We've got to make commitments to our neighborhoods and cities bigger than vision and emotion; we need to covenant with others to grow roots in our cities or we will continue to create baggage for those who are already skeptical of us.

EMBRACE THE TENSION

Growing roots always involves tension. Jonathan Wilson-Hartgrove says, "From the very beginning, those who have practiced stability in the way of Jesus have acknowledged a healthy tension between commitment to a place and the call to go elsewhere."[1] Not only do we wrestle between our desire for roots and wings; we wrestle with God's desires for us. There's a whole world out there in need of the liberating love of Jesus. How can I go about choosing who needs it more? There are cracks everywhere, and we have only one life to expend. The thought can be maddening.

A large part of this tension is a natural pull between two places and the cultures that represent them. The people I observe who have the hardest time adapting to new cultures have only lived in one place or one region; they can be considered monocultural. Monocultural people are vulnerable to "cultural snobbery," the assumption that their cultural background is the baseline by which other cultures should be judged. The adjusted bicultural person, in contrast, has gotten used to another place and the culture inherent in it.[2] Our understanding of what is "normal" or "right" is necessarily stretched by exposure to unfamiliar cultures. To become locals in a new place we must fight through the assumption that the views and flavor of life where we grew up were exclusively right.

Another tension we live in is moving from owners of our lives to stewards. Our theology and philosophy have taken a wrong turn when we begin to think it's all up to us. The reality that brokenness is all around me previously left me feeling paralyzed, but now it reminds me there is work to do everywhere. From the richest neighborhoods in your city to the other side of the tracks, Jesus is inviting us to join the process of his Kingdom coming. You can serve right where you're at. All you need to do is be faithful and intentionally present in the name of Jesus. How glorious that God has work for all of us to do right in our front yards, relationships, and towns!

Growing wings with no eye on the ground beneath our feet us is an uncalculated risk; the grass is almost never greener on the other side of the fence. But staying on this side of the fence can be even scarier, if for no other reason than it might not equate to success in others' minds. I believe, as followers of Jesus, growing roots is a risk we simply have to take. It's not easy; my life has been turned on its side in some areas and completely upside-down in others, but I don't want to go back to right-side-up. Our rhythms, parties, days off, desires, and friendships have all been affected significantly. It's a daily journey of dying to some of my own expectations and habits, but a sprouting in ways I never hoped for.

HOW OUR PARTIES HAVE CHANGED

We had no idea who these people in our kitchen were. I gave my wife that look that means, "Who invited these random strangers? Do they live in our neighborhood or are they friends of friends? Had they happened upon the wrong party?" We shook their hands and awkwardly asked, "So, who do you know around here?"

It turned out their son had brought them. Our boys were kindergarten buddies. We had made flyers for the party and handed them out to neighbors, and without us knowing, Manny had taken a stack of the flyers and handed them out to his class. Now here I was, talking to a repo man and repo woman who had joined us for a beautiful night of laughs, holiday junk food, and a carol sing. They would soon become curb buddies with us for Free Coffee Friday.

I was blown away and incredibly proud of my son. At five years old he understood that our Christmas parties should be open to everyone in our lives. Sometimes our kids naturally "get" Kingdom life better than we do.

Our parties used to consist of our friends who looked like us and believed what we believed—family and friends we had a lot in common with. Then we made an intentional shift to invite everyone in our orbit. I just have to laugh sometimes when I wonder what we've gotten ourselves into. Our parties now routinely involve a few perfect strangers and others on the margins of our lives, waiting for the right moment to connect. I never have any idea who is going to show up and how it's all going to work, but somehow it always does. This nearly open invitation into our lives and homes creates a beautifully connective space that I referred to earlier as collective overlap. It's a ride, and it's awesome.

We started to see parties as an excuse to connect with new people *and* to take old relationships deeper—a place to understand our God who invites people to a banquet feast where the food never runs out and the well never runs dry. I never viewed parties as a theological statement until I noticed how strategically Jesus used parties as opportunities to make theological statements of who is welcome, who is worth risking your reputation for.

In Luke 14 Jesus tells the parable of the banquet feast:

> A man once gave a great banquet and invited many. And at the time for the banquet he sent his servant to say to those who had been invited, "Come, for everything is now ready." But they all alike began to make excuses. The first said to him, "I have bought a field, and I must go out and see it. Please have me excused." And another said, "I have bought five yoke of oxen, and I go to examine them. Please have me excused." And another said, "I have married a wife, and therefore I cannot come." So the servant came and reported these things to his master. Then the master of the house became angry and said to his servant, "Go out quickly to the streets and lanes of the city, and bring in the poor and crippled and blind and lame." And the servant said, "Sir, what you commanded has been done, and still there is room." And the master said to the servant, "Go out to the highways and hedges and compel people to come in, that my house may be filled." LUKE 14:16-23

The first thing to note from this parable is the age-old plight of busyness. Let's not blame Western culture for our busyness; it's right here in the pages of Scripture. Don't get discouraged when people turn you down and seem to be terminally unavailable. Keep inviting them, and look to find others who want to accept your invitation.

This story also shows the deep intention of the Father to fill up his house with those who are available and hungry— not merely with those who are most like us. Our parties used to resemble Elks Club gatherings, but now they feel like a hospital room with a revolving door after a baby is born: everyone gets in who wants a peek. I realize that might sound exhausting to you. That's where the risk comes in.

STAYING, EVEN UNTO DEATH

The risk of roots is this: you get invited into the mess, and you have to stay to clean up. There is brokenness all around us. Faithful presence will take us a few steps past the borders of comfort. But you will encounter the gospel there.

In the case of some early Christians, the mess of staying led them to death. During the plagues sweeping across Europe, people would rush out to escape, leaving loved ones behind, out of fear of imminent death. The gospel response of many of the early Christians, in contrast, was to stay and care for the sick. Around AD 260 Dionysius wrote a letter sharing the "heroic nursing efforts of local Christians."

The heathen behaved in the very opposite way.
At the first onset of the disease, they pushed the
sufferers away and fled from their dearest, throwing

them into the roads before they were dead and
treated unburied corpses as dirt, hoping thereby
to avert the spread of and contagion of the fatal
disease.[3]

Many who had been left for dead simply needed basic care
and hygiene to survive the plague, and Rodney Stark notes
that many Christians (though not all) built an immunity to
the disease; meanwhile, "its full impact fell on the heathen."[4]

Ironically the Christian movement grew during the
plague. After being nursed back to health through this incredible act of self-effacing love, many people gave their lives
to Jesus and joined this community; whereas one story had
left them abandoned in the name of fear, the Christian story
had led to a demonstration of costly love in the name of
Jesus.[5]

The actions and faith of the early Christians became
known far and wide as a charity to be emulated. Later, "the
emperor Julian launched a campaign to institute pagan chari-
ties in an effort to match the Christians."[6] This pattern continues today. Some local and state governments are asking
groups to mimic churches in facilitating foster care and adoption of children who need homes.

Kent Brantly is a physician who, during medical school,
decided to serve the underserved by bringing his skills to
countries with very few resources. Shortly after relocating
from Indiana and joining the staff of a Liberian mission hospital, Ebola hit like a tidal wave. Brantly could have left, but

his faith beckoned him to stay. Many criticized his decision; one person referred publicly to this risk as "idiotic."[7] Brantly said this: "We couldn't abandon [Liberia] in a time when they had their greatest need."[8] Brantly has addressed the US president and Congress regarding the effects of Ebola, which he ultimately contracted. Through proper medical care, God spared his life.[9]

When popular wisdom says to run from danger, boredom, disease, or meaninglessness, the gospel often beckons us to stay. Sometimes the best opportunities to love others involve staying in the midst of fear. My friends Kory and Alli decided to move into a rough neighborhood of South Bend, Indiana. They saw the cracks there. Although they had nearly nothing in common with the people in the neighborhood, their hearts broke for the kids growing up there. Over the past several years they have become a safe house for play, learning, meals, mentorship, and hanging around. They have committed to raising their kids in a hard place, because they believe the gospel compels them to. They are faithfully embodying and proclaiming Jesus, and helping young people fight the lies of hopelessness in the neighborhood.

SIMPLE AND REALLY HARD

All the ways my family has sought faithful presence in our neighborhood have been simple, but really hard. We've not employed any methods I would call innovative. Free Coffee Friday on the corner started out of a desire to connect with people once a week in one consistent place. We figured wherever there are parents there is a desire for connection and a need for caffeine. It's really simple: meet us here every Friday when school is in session, just before school starts and awhile after. It's also really hard—hard to get out of bed early on my day off. I fight the temptation to let it slip for a week. It can be hard to see the gospel impact of connecting with these people. It can be hard to keep showing up. If we had called it quits, however, we would have missed out on all the relationships we've developed and the spiritual victories we've seen. A few others have picked up the idea and are doing this in front of their schools and in their neighborhoods.

We are out there rain, shine, or snow. It's particularly hard when it snows. One day I was angry at the school district for not calling school off due to the very icy roads and South Pole windchill. The conditions were terrible. A friend and I stood on the curb, sure we would have to drink all the coffee ourselves. That wasn't far from the truth. We wound up pushing four cars up the hill that morning. This journey has been fun and fruitful along the way, but it certainly hasn't been easy.

It's easy to start things, but hard to maintain them. You are going to need to make a commitment to anything involving faithful presence. There's no way around it. It doesn't happen overnight, and the trick is to stick to it long enough to see the impact.

I have a friend who leads a skate ministry in my city. It's not an easy group to focus on, and he has supported his ministry habit in various ways over his years of ministry. He was recently offered his dream ministry position in a place where a skate ministry is well established; they don't have cold winters, and his family could finally live off his salary. On the plane home, he knew he needed to stay in our city and make a recommitment here. Just months later they moved into their dream: an indoor skate park, where they could have more influence on the skate community.

Foreign missionaries often spend several discouraging years in a country before one person commits their life to Jesus. Expect similar things on your home turf. Lives get busy, and time will fly. If we aren't intentional about regular and relational times of staying well in the face of discouragement, it simply won't happen. When you commit to something, the biggest risk you will take is committing to simply showing up.

Staying is most powerful when going is the most logical thing to do. After Hurricane Katrina I led one of many teams that went down to help the rebuilding process. We went to a small rural strip south of New Orleans; the damage was devastating. There were cars in trees and huge shrimp boats blocking the road into town. Some of the families we met had been there for generations; they had no plan of leaving. But many people thought twice about staying. I remember gutting a church building, and after our work one day a local pastor told us he had reached out to the church's pastor and received no calls back; the whole congregation was probably gone for good.

While I couldn't imagine rebuilding my home and church

building from the ground up, I also couldn't fathom how a church would simply disband. Would anyone from the congregation return? This was the biggest opportunity they had seen in fifty years to serve their community, and by leaving they might never experience the fruit from this terrible situation. The building became a storage facility and command center for another church in town, who stayed to rebuild homes long after FEMA had left.

THE TERRIBLE MASTERPIECE OF PROXIMITY

Closeness brings up a whole new set of issues. We've all waded through frustration with neighbors, sat awkwardly at a community table, or overheard private phone conversations. Proximity can be beautiful, but it can also be uncomfortable and challenging.

Living a life of mission is hardest when you have nowhere to hide. Proximity allows others to view pieces of our lives through a glass house. Family, friends, and neighbors see us in our grumpiest moments. Here's the good news, though: Others have nowhere to hide either. The people who saw you at your worst are also a glance away when you mow a neighbor's yard, hug a coworker who is still grieving her miscarriage, or watch a ragtag bunch file into your home for a party. They will get to see you ask for forgiveness and experience grace. Those closest to us will taste the saltiness of Jesus; they will find refuge in his light. There is nowhere for it to hide.

A few months back, I had one of those moments when I wish I could have hidden. I hate painting walls. Period. To this day I'm not sure why I hate it so much. I'd rather follow my daughter and her friends around at a mall all day than paint walls in my house. One day I was painting and feeling more than a bit cranky, so I went outside to take a break and found my wife talking to a neighbor. She had likely left the house because I was being such a grump. I had the choice to act like the perfect husband or admit I had been acting like a cranky six-year-old. I chose the latter.

"I really hate painting," I said. "I have such a lousy attitude when I have to paint." The neighbor looked shocked that I would share that. We all need others to see the beauty in us, but we also have a need for others to see the cracks in who we are. Proximity allows others around us to experience beauty, generosity, failure, and grace *in us*.

SERVING AND RECIPROCATION

After entering our neighborhood and building relationships with a serving posture, we began to develop friendships. This was exciting. *We're finally getting somewhere!* I thought. Then we experienced a strange next step: being served in return. Honestly, I had not previously had many sustained relationships with people far from God, so this reciprocity surprised me. Suddenly our family was being served in meaningful ways. It was humbling to receive.

Even in our acts of service we can hold a posture of strength. It sounds strange, but when you start serving, you will need to exercise the humility to receive from others. One of the strangest risks you will deal with is reciprocation.

Here's a progression you will likely experience if you serve those around you long enough:

SERVICE → RELATIONSHIP → RECIPROCATION

Service is our point of entry. We aim solely at serving others around us. We are focused, ready for the challenge, and not expecting anything back from anyone. It's a full surrender to loving people. The seed is in the ground.

In the *relationship* stage we start to understand the people around us—both the good and the bad—and we experience meaningful interaction with them. As we serve, we hear their stories and share laughs with them; our interactions feel less like serving and more like friendship. While it still requires dedication, we find ourselves looking forward to being around the people we've chosen to serve. The roots begin to grow.

Reciprocation is the beautiful threshold where relationships blossom and others begin to serve with us and sometimes actually serve us. People around us catch a vision, pitch in, and participate in something bigger than themselves. When you are in need, they step up and do for you what you've modeled for them. They bless you and it surprises you. This can be hard to accept, because there's a stubborn strength in serving others. In this phase our hearts are deeply moved by the Father when we experience their love as an extension of God's love.

Once we are in true relationship, every human is wired

to serve. Ephesians 2:10 tells us we are "[God's] workman-ship" with a destiny to serve. We now enjoy the blessings of invitations for the big game, offers to babysit our kids for a date night, neighbors who mow our lawn when we're on vacation, and unexpected birthday gifts. Try to determine which of these three phases you are in, and be honest with yourself about the challenges of your phase. In almost all scenarios you will eventually find the accidental blessing of reciprocation in a caring, loving community. But never stop blessing those around you. It will cost you something to stay well in relationships.

If staying is an investment, don't be surprised when the return on these investments is not only spiritual but rela-tional and physical also.

FIGHT, FLIGHT, OR FLOURISH

We have three options in our relationships and places: fight, flight, or flourish. Fight or flight are referred to in counsel-ing. Experts in counseling can spot them easily when conflict arises.

A woman from our missional community got a door slammed on her and some colorful language thrown her way when she showed up sharing about a food drive we were doing after a devastating fire in our city. It had very little to do with the lady at the door. This impulse to fight is easy to spot on the surface but tough to diagnose. Someone in close proximity will fight if they feel it's their only option. At times, neighbors and friends have employed this mechanism when they didn't want me as close as I had invited them. I used to take this as an insult; now I simply take it as a warning.

People take flight through avoidance. This is easy in our culture today. It ranges from unfriending someone on social media, to acting too busy to engage in relationships at work, to driving in and out of the garage for weeks to avoid conversation. People can become masters at planning their avoidance strategies. Flight is the most common reaction I see today, and the easiest way out. I have caught myself hiding in my house to dodge a long conversation with a needy neighbor or acting busy when a school parent is walking toward me as I'm picking up my kids. We have to fight off these temptations along the journey of faithful presence. When we choose flight we eliminate any chance of impact.

Relationships can only flourish when people embrace tension for a long period of time. We need boundaries, but we also need to give our time away to others as a gift. Many followers of Jesus today are overwhelmed with maintaining their life, and so their service to others is underwhelming. We need family time, but we also need to shift our view of the family of God to become broader and welcome others in. We need time away on vacations, but we also need to learn to share relaxed leisure time in our yards and living rooms. We will have conflict, but we need to choose to resolve conflict and serve others instead of running. We will all get annoyed and hurt by those closest to us, but we need to choose to forgive and lean into our relationships.

The first time our neighbors went on vacation, their lawn

looked like a lion sanctuary. I wondered if they really needed their lawn mowed, or if they would take it as an insult. I decided to go for it. It only took ten minutes and I soon forgot about it. After returning from vacation, our neighbor came over to our house and said, "No one has ever mowed our lawn before. Thank you so much!"

We flourish when we embrace the opportunity to make ordinary choices in ordinary moments. As followers of Jesus, perhaps this is where we will shine the most. We need not wait for a crisis moment or a tragedy in someone's life. Walk out the door today and take the next right step.

FROM TOURISTS TO PILGRIMS

Moving from winged people to rooted people is more than a strategy change; it's a posture change. Leonard Hjalmarson suggests we make the change from tourists to pilgrims. The more we invest in those around us, the more we leave relational tourism behind.[10]

On the road from tourists to pilgrims, I believe we must pass through two other stages.

TOURIST → PESSIMIST → LOCAL → PILGRIM

The tourist stage. The tourist stage is marked by fascination. A place is new, and everything about it feels fresh and interesting. Tourists care very little about the hard realities of the place; they care more about having pleasant weather and seeing all the sites. Tourists are consumers of places. When tourists come to my town, they spend a little time and money and move on. They don't come during the lull of the off-season, and you can't depend on them. Tourists don't change places; they consume them.

The pessimist stage. After the tourist stage, you will experience some disenchantment. The honeymoon is over, and you realize it won't be easy to sustain life here. After all, there's the need for a job to sustain you financially and the stress that relationships inevitably bring. When you get to the end of the tourist stage with a place, you realize you will have to fight to stay engaged and perhaps to even make a living there. You entertain the notion of leaving: "It will be easier back home or in another place where people will respect me." You will get frustrated by the barriers to the gospel there.[11] Often the reasons for leaving a place are very natural; your uniqueness is not appreciated here like it was "back home." Paul Hiebert says, "In our own society we know who we are because we hold offices, degrees, and memberships in different groups. In this new setting our old identity is gone. We must start all over again to become somebody."[12] While each of these difficulties has a kernel of truth, they are mostly lies and needy self-talk we need to push through.

"The first year or two," Hiebert says, "is crucial in our adaptation to a new culture. How we adjust during this time will color our ministry for the rest of our lives."[13] How you start your journey into place matters. I have seen people come with the heart to learn and have seen people adapt more in two years than others have in ten years. Taking the posture of a learner for the long haul can make the first few years in a new place a training ground and a solidifying season.

The local stage. Those who push through the pessimist stage will eventually arrive at the local stage. You understand the culture and rhythm of the people, and they begin to understand you. Depending on how cross-cultural your place is, they might not even notice you came from the outside. You are comfortable having a sustained presence there, and others in the tourist and pessimist stage might even take comfort in seeing your journey to becoming a local. This is a crucial stage where followers of Jesus can begin to have a long-term impact on others. You are trusted here, and you begin to have some of the same skepticism about tourists counting the cost in that place.

The pilgrim stage. With work and desire, eventually you can arrive at the pilgrim stage. This is where you move beyond comfortability to live with determined longevity in a place. This is when you make true sacrifices to stay there. You might also deny potentially exciting opportunities to leave. You become known for loving your place and working for its welfare. As in a mature marriage, you actually love your place more than you did in the tourist phase when everything seemed perfect. You have fought through the hard realities, the desire to leave, and the wanderlust to chase the dream somewhere else.

In Genesis 2:15 Adam and Eve were given the mandate to work the garden and keep it, to cultivate the land.[14] I believe the keeping of our land can be a joyful task where we meet

God in ways we never could have imagined. The posture of a pilgrim can lead us into life's alleyways as we pray for God's Kingdom to come in our places and we join in watching it happen before our eyes.

North American church ministry needs to move gracefully from a posture of conquering and converting and instead join a joyful ~~pilgrimage~~ CURATING to the spots God has placed us. Certainly the gospel reveals that Jesus is the conqueror and converter, not us; he has conquered our sin, and he alone has the power to save. We, on the other hand, are *more* than conquerors in Jesus. We are stewards of his gifts, caretakers in his fields. As we leave conquering and converting to Jesus, we find ourselves knee-deep in the soil he has allowed us to cultivate. This is what God has wired us to be: fully present blessings to those around us, stewarding the great gifts of God.

QUESTIONS FOR REFLECTION AND DISCUSSION

What are some challenging, but potentially fruitful, relationships you need to reengage?

Which of the three phases—service, relationship, or reciprocation—describes your interactions with those around you? What is most challenging about this phase?

Would you describe yourself more as a tourist, pessimist, local, or pilgrim of your place? What is your next right step toward the posture of a rooted pilgrim?

SALT, LIGHT, AND SHOVELS

"A key issue for any group willing to embrace the risk and adventure of mission is to dare to believe that they have been sent to stay home."

MICHAEL FROST AND ALAN HIRSCH, *THE FAITH OF LEAP*

"Learn to love the people around you, see them with the eyes of God, and accept them as God does."

SR. AQUINATA BOCKMANN

"Both people and place remain at the center of God's purposes."

LEONARD HJALMARSON, *NO HOME LIKE PLACE*

I WAS GRAVELY disappointed we were heading to Pittsburgh for our two-week ministry immersion trip in the dead of winter. I was envisioning Phoenix, Orlando, or Southern California. During those two weeks we met many leaders living on mission in traditional and nontraditional ways—from liturgical churches to tattoo parlors to business networks. One pastor we connected with during this time was named John. We spent some time experiencing his church. I was unfamiliar with his tradition, and I struggled to connect to him and his story.

John and his wife graciously invited seventeen of us to

their home for dinner one cold night. I will never forget his wife's stew and the story John told that night. While we were scattered all over his living room, John told us about the moment his ministry in Pittsburgh truly began.

A man named Sam Shoemaker declared a daring vision for Pittsburgh many years ago. He dreamed of Pittsburgh becoming "as famous for God as for steel." In 1967 two ministry leaders, burdened by Sam's dream, gathered on a prominent hill overlooking the city to pray God would do something unique there. Reid Carpenter, a man working with youth throughout the city, asked, "Do you love Jesus? Do you love Pittsburgh? Are you willing to commit yourself to remain in this place for fifteen to twenty years to seek the Lord's will here?"[1]

These leaders were not just interested in making Pittsburgh a better place to live. These two men began to talk about a theology of place years before the term would become used elsewhere. They knew if God's Kingdom was to manifest all over creation, surely their city was included. Compelled by their vision for God's work in the city, John visited Pittsburgh and committed to join them the next year. People began referring to this commitment to prayer and revival as the Pittsburgh Offensive.

The outgrowth of the Pittsburgh Offensive was a movement of followers of Jesus from many different streams who made the name of Jesus known—from high school students in struggling areas to influential businesspeople in high-rises. Through God's grace many people came to know Jesus, incredible ecumenical and strategic unity developed among churches, over twenty-five ministries were founded, youth programs were formed, racial reconciliation was addressed, housing initiatives were developed, and healthcare and education were revitalized. A man named Don James even helped to start externally focused small groups in median spaces, strangely similar to today's missional communities, that translated Jesus for those who wouldn't walk into a church building. They were doing it long before the big conferences and bestselling Christian books. They grabbed on and gave their lives fully to God's work in their city. Talk about missional!

God brought some incredible gospel leaders to Pittsburgh in that season. You probably wouldn't recognize most of these men and women as national figures. Perhaps they were so focused on putting their heads down and bringing God's glory to their city that they didn't have time for much else.

Much of what happened in Pittsburgh came from transplants who made a commitment to stay and work for the good of the city. And yet despite all these amazing leaders, the Pittsburgh Offensive was a slow burn. Much of the fire came from the hearts of transformed high school and college students, who accepted the challenge to stay rather than leave, and to work for the welfare of the city.

These movement leaders realized they must stay long enough in the city to see young people transition into prominent city leaders. In his book describing this city movement, *Taking the Gospel to the Point*,[2] Michael J. Sider-Rose says,

"Their strategy of creating a teen-through-adult ministry could only succeed, they reasoned, if Christians lived in one place long enough to guide a new generation of leaders into maturity."[3] This realization led them to join what God was already doing in their city.

When I met him, John Guest had been in Pittsburgh for thirty-seven years. As a naive, zealous college student bound for ministry, I will never forget the gut punch I received that first time I ever heard about a theology of place. I had never considered that staying forth could trump going forth and unlock God's work in a city.

John later wrote me, "The work the Lord did in those days continues to expand and be strong in his grace, with a new generation of leadership following along! God bless as you 'go for it' in Colorado." He's still the same John that arrived on the scene ready and willing to commit to God becoming more famous than steel in his city.

If we are going to see similar gospel movements in the places we live, staying must become the new going. It's time to start making commitments to our cities instead of just to jobs and houses. A friend shared with me a similar impulse from Brad Feld, one of the founders of TechStars in Boulder, Colorado. He composed the Boulder Thesis, which calls on local entrepreneurs to make a twenty-year commitment to Boulder, and to renew it every day. If tech leaders are encouraging people to recommit to their city each day, how much more should we, as ambassadors of God's Kingdom work, be making that commitment to our places!

PEOPLE OF THE SHOVEL

As we embrace the call to be salt and light in our places, our weapon of choice must change. Instead of the combative presence Christians are known for, it's time for us to become people of the shovel. We need to develop a reputation as loving and committed champions of our communities. Instead of being distracted by taking new ground for Jesus, we need to shift our focus to digging into *this* ground for Jesus.

There are community champions who are faithfully present all around us. They are quiet heroes. Rebecca, a mother of a disabled daughter, takes time to serve others with lesser means than her. A pastor named Lewis has been developing other pastors in my city for years, leaving a wake of faithful church leaders behind him. Seth and Angela always seem to have a group around them whom they have pulled into their lives from hard situations. A man named Joe bought a house near the parish his family was called to serve; he didn't take a check from the church for over twenty years. Joe is a software engineer who pastors a church that is more than 50 percent Cambodian, with many homeless in their congregation. A friend started a business in a tough area of my city and has had organizations seek his opinion on how we can make headway against hard issues here.

Other people in my city have grabbed the shovel and gotten to work. A church adopted their struggling neighborhood school. A church planter moved to the hard part of the city where he knew he couldn't support his family, got a job, and stayed. A schoolteacher intentionally stayed in a poorly rated school instead of moving to a better school district with better pay in order to address the severe needs there. A family decided to take in young men who had no place to go. A small group dared to identify one area they could affect in their city and filled many cracks there. An employee spent lunch once a week with a new coworker. A church has had a faithful missions partnership with the same country for twenty years. A mom of four is committed to taking care of her neighbor's special-needs child so she can get a break. A pastor turned down a job opportunity at a bigger suburban church to stay and minister in a struggling small church. A church committed to measuring their success in community involvement instead of people in their seats. A church member stayed to minister in his church while fighting off the boredom that tempted him to leave. An older church voted to give their building to a young church plant that could serve the neighbors and continue the mission in that parish.

These are some of my heroes. Who are your heroes? They will shape our narratives. Who are the ones reminding you to be faithful right now, right here in the guts of life? The ordinary heroes are the ones who have taken the next right step. They might not have a mission statement or five-year vision, but they are faithful enough to trust God and act. Like them, we must fight through feeling overwhelmed by the ocean of opportunities and obstacles, and focus on taking the next step toward faithful presence.

Unearthing these stories of courageous ordinaries involves some careful excavation. Many of these folks are hard at work, busy digging their roots and wholeheartedly distracted by faithfulness. Most of them don't think they are doing anything notable. If the only stories followers of Jesus are hearing are the ones from paid church leaders on a stage, we are in trouble. We need to become detectives of faithful missional presence and tattle on people for doing good. Look for the shovel-wielding heroes shaping the witness of the church today. They may never write books or speak on large stages, but they are dwelling well.

BEAUTIFUL LIMITATIONS

The gospel makes the most sense in proximity. Perhaps this is because proximity invites us to taste what Jesus tasted in coming to earth. He was born into a family, lived in a small geographic space, and entered the mess of all things human except sin itself. Jamie Arpin-Ricci says, "The incarnation was God choosing to locate himself very physically in a time and place. He accepted the limits of 'the least of these' to genuinely be one of the people he dwelt among. By doing the same, we not only connect with others, but with Christ as well."[4]

Jesus came to this earth in weakness, yet we have learned to avoid it. At times Jesus chose to embrace obscurity, yet we abhor it. Limits give us the illusion of weakness. We are limited to being in one place at a time. We drift away from being emotionally present when we lock into our phones. Over time, however, we come to terms with our physical limits. Time limits allow us to be present with people doing

[handwritten margin note: INCARNATION GOD IN PROXIMITY]

very ordinary things. Mature followers of Jesus realize limits are a beautiful thing. Those without limits simply cannot be faithfully present where they are placed.

There was power in the limits of Jesus. He conveyed power in his local questions, his local conversations, his neighborly glances, his friendly meals. Jesus met local needs and effectively "wasted" his time developing a small band of misfits. Every one of those powerful expressions of the ministry of Jesus involves one thing: presence. Jesus lived with intention, limits, and an unrelenting focus on being present. I often wonder: If Jesus lived in a busy, metropolitan city today, how would he live? I'm not sure where and how he would spend his time, but I can bet you he wouldn't be the busiest guy in the neighborhood.

FROM FORTRESS TO HUB

Imagine getting invited over for dinner by a world-class chef. After attending one of her seminars and watching her effortlessly prepare delicacies on TV, you anxiously accept the invite. You are ready to have your cooking transformed forever. Much to your surprise, there is nothing out in the kitchen when you arrive. Her home smells like mothballs. After some small talk she heats up a few Hot Pockets, and you eat on the couch with the TV on. It turns out cooking is just her job, and she is too tired to cook at home.

Christians can function the same way. Our homes can become fortresses away from the stress and worries of the world. We can be so busy attending church events, gathering with other Christians, and teaching a Bible study that we want to just collapse on the couch in our time off. If people who don't know Jesus enter our homes, we have the chance to immerse them in a loving family and community. I hope they smell the aroma of Christ, not the mothballs of stress and discontentment. If our homes begin to function as castles, our kids, friends, and neighbors will never get to experience how the gospel tastes. How sad would it be if our neighbors only know us as the ones who drive to church on weekends, but never bring the gospel home with us.

Salt and light won't spill out of our homes if people don't encounter Jesus through us on the sidewalk and in our living rooms. If we raise kids in a house where everyone is welcome, our kids will see our theology in action—the risks we take to love others instead of fearing cultural differences. They will get a true sense of hospitality as we prepare good meals and wash dishes. I will never forget one Easter dinner my parents hosted when I was growing up. Instead of heading home and heating up leftovers, they invited an array of college students and singles to our home. My mom had prepared a feast expecting people to accept a last-minute invitation. After eating far too much, everyone started getting tired, so my parents declared a group nap time. I woke up to about fifteen people, some of whom I barely knew, on the floor and couches in our family room. That was over twenty years ago, and I will never forget the theology lesson I got that day: everyone is welcome at this banquet table.

DWELL WELL

In *The Rise of Christianity* sociologist Rodney Stark spends over two hundred pages researching this question: "How did a tiny and obscure messianic movement from the edge of the Roman Empire dislodge classical paganism and become the dominant faith of Western civilization?"[5] After exploring various contributing factors to its growth, his final conclusion was this:

> The primary means of its growth was through the united and motivated efforts of the growing numbers of Christian believers, who invited their friends, relatives and neighbors to share the "good news."[6]

While human empires rose and fell, the gospel exploded through simplicity in close proximity. A similar explosion is accessible to us if we commit ourselves to our relationships, our neighborhoods, and our cities.

STAY IN RELATIONSHIP

There are people right around us with whom we already share common ground, common ideas, common emotions, common loves, and common rhythms. Just like the early church, we live in both physical and relational proximity to many people who need to know the life-altering love of Jesus. The relationship between dwelling well in proximity to others and proclaiming the name of Jesus should be inseparable. Sean Benesh says, "Presence does not negate proclamation, instead it empowers it. Presence gives proclamation legs to stand on. By becoming rooted and established in place we earn the right and the credibility to be heard."[7]

I have been slowly walking with my friend Matt for nearly ten years. About five years ago God prompted me to reengage in intentional relationship with Matt. He doesn't understand my life as a follower of Jesus or a pastor, but he likes hanging out with me, and he loves my family. I have earned a lot of credibility with him. I'm guessing you have people like Matt in your life—friends or family members who don't understand you but respect you. Giving Jesus a proper introduction can take some time, often years of committed friendship. When we uproot we miss the opportunity to see what God might do in these folks. Chances are there are people you are already in relationship with whom you could reengage with today.

There have been seasons where Matt and I have spent a lot of time together and seasons where he was extremely busy. Over time I have been chipping away at his vulnerability. I brought Matt along this year on my annual dudes' wilderness trip, and we had the deepest conversations we have ever had. He told me about wounds from his father and feelings of failure in areas of his life. Sometimes you don't need to change what you're doing; you just need to be patient.

Matt doesn't long for marriage, but he told me he would get married if he could have a relationship like my wife and I have. He comes to every party he can possibly attend at my house, because he loves all my friends. He told me, "Your friends are the most genuine people I know." He asks me to refer renters to him because he knows he can trust Christians to keep his place looking nice. Matt has tried to peel back the layers of my life several times, asking me why my friends and marriage are winsome. "Matt," I've responded, "I don't know what else to tell you. It's not about me; it's about Jesus."

People around us should be baffled by our lives. Michael Frost boldly asks, "Is your life questionable?"[8] If we live a Jesus life, we should be an anomaly to those around us. I long for the day when Matt comes to know Jesus, but I will still love him and invest in him if he doesn't.

The desire for freshness can draw us away from the stability of longevity. We often unintentionally trade in our old friends or places for new ones like we would trade in our old car for a sleeker one. Upgrading relationships can be hurtful; reengaging relationships can bring fruitful depth. But by the time most of us get to a place of depth in relationships, we are bored and considering disengagement. This is the time to stay engaged and lean in closer!

On our first date, my now-wife Julie got a call while we were driving to hear some live music. She talked for a minute or so and began to motion at me as if to say, "I'll tell you later, it's important, I'm really sorry." About five minutes into her conversation, I figured out she was talking to an inmate. *Who is this girl?* I thought. *She's talking to a dude in prison while we're on our first date! What kind of move is that?*

After twenty minutes she said good-bye and hung up. I was completely baffled by her constant and loyal heart.

Truthfully, I was more attracted to her after her explanation and glad she had taken the call.

My wife is far better at staying well in relationships than I am. For her it's an impulse, and for me it's a discipline. I need constant reminders, whereas it seems to run through her bloodstream. My wife has cared for our friend Nate, the inmate from that call, for over fifteen years now. While some have been drawn to Nate and his story for brief seasons, my wife never quit. She kept writing him. She kept leaning in. Her constant care for him has profoundly changed Nate's life, her life, and my life.

Not only would Nate call Julie his longest standing friend, he has granted us power of attorney. We've sat with him many times, eating snacks and playing games in the meeting room in the prison three hours away. We've helped him get documents and arrange the schooling he's receiving behind bars. Julie hasn't done anything amazing or extraordinary; she has just stayed in relationship really well. I will never forget how humbled we were when Nate sent us a large sum of money for our adoption. We knew how little he made for each hour of work, and we were blown away and a bit teary-eyed.

STAY IN YOUR NEIGHBORHOOD

My friend Dave Runyon has experienced a hard and beautiful journey into incarnational ministry. He says, "When we are intentional about forming relationships based on proximity, we are stretched to know and love people who are very different than us."[9] I call this stretching process "relational immersion." Our neighborhoods are full of people who appear to be nothing like us, but at the core are fellow humans with pain, joy, stress, fear, and generosity, just like us. When we immerse ourselves in relationships, we peel away the layers and find the humanity and commonalities. If we can engage our neighborhoods and make the commitment to stay for the long haul, we can get ready for God to do great things.

I don't know how many times I've heard the advice, "Don't buy a home; it ties you down." Couple this statement with the number of friends I know who have had their homes foreclosed on, and I was not excited about buying a home. Not one bit. I thought we were living the dream in our long-term rental agreement—until our landlords started talking about us moving out and flipping the place. I began to hate the thought of moving out. God had taught us so much here, neighbors were becoming friends, and I could not separate my practice of the gospel as a pastor, a neighbor, and a friend anymore. I began a wrestling match with God.

The biggest question we asked during that season of wrestling with God was, "Are mortgages missional?" Some people argue that we need to stay mobile, ready to respond should God lead us in a different direction. A mortgage can tie us down for decades; moreover, there are worries associated with homeownership, and it's easy to turn inward and focus on our little fortress. Critics of homeownership might also talk about the temptation it can add to bow the knee to the idol of security. Jesus and the disciples, they remind us, traveled with no extra suitcase or stash of food; the Father took care of their needs. These critics tend to forget that Jesus instructed his wandering disciples to make quick connections with a person of peace rooted in the community (Luke 10:1-12). But overall, they make a pretty good case.

Others argue that it's hard to have a lasting impact for Jesus in our neighborhoods if we aren't in it for the long haul. There's a trust factor to relationships, and this trust doesn't come overnight, so we need to pay our dues (as we pay our mortgage) in order to be a Kingdom hub in our neighborhood. They might say we need to be *of* a certain place and a certain people in order to truly gain trust and become missionaries. They might emphasize an exiled Judah in Jeremiah 29 digging in and building homes, planting gardens and working for the good of that city. Overall, they also make a pretty good case.

There's no easy answer here. Where you choose to plant yourself is a big decision. We have a limited quantity of time, money, and energy here on this earth, and how we spend it matters deeply to God.

The biggest danger here, I believe, is justifying the biggest purchase of our lives in the name of God. Close behind is the danger of imposing our answer to this question on others. In some cases buying a home is incredibly missional, and in other cases it can be a self-seeking way to move out of a perfectly good house just to keep up with the Joneses. Houses cost a lot of money, and mortgages can cost a lot of worry, but the financial commitment can help keep you committed to the place and the people around it. Wrestle through this question with the Father and those you trust, and see what God says.

Last year, after a series of open doors, we signed the infamous stack of papers that accompany a mortgage. Now we are semipermanent here. We don't just tell neighbors, "Our door is open"; we tell them, "We'll be behind this door for a long time." Yes, we have lost a little bit of flexibility and had to take on more responsibility. We have also made a statement to our neighbors that we're staying.

Jamie Arpin-Ricci gives this needed reminder: "It takes many years to truly become rooted in a neighborhood. Do not give too much attention to 'outcomes' that churches often ask for."[10] Real life in a neighborhood will force you to fight your urge to meet number quotas, pursue large goals, and move too quickly. You may wrestle with this on a regular basis as you push against unrealistic metrics. Effective ministry in our places has very little to do with measuring people and a lot to do with years, tears, and posture.

STAY IN CITIES

I recently had a conversation with a barista as I was waiting for my drink. I overheard her saying, "I'm really starting to love this city"; that kicked off a long conversation with her about what she loved to do, what she sees changing in our city, and what kind of community she had formed around her. She said she would probably end up staying.

Then I dropped the bomb. "What would it take for you

to stay for twenty years?" She got nervous. It was obvious she hadn't thought that far out. It was as if I had asked her to give up drinking coffee or remove her tattoos.

Most of us are in this zone; we have a crush on the place we live, but we haven't made a commitment. Like the barista, most people think of staying in a city as an exchange. If _____ (insert your place here) can provide me _____ (insert your community dream here), I will stay. If not, I will find another place that can. It sounds like the prevalent view of marriage drifting through our culture today. I hope we begin to understand a theology of place that is more of a covenant than a crush. It's not a sin to leave a place, and we might not end up staying forty years, but we must spend the time we have as if we are going to stay.

At some point everyone thinks about moving away. Often this is for legitimate reasons like a job or proximity to family. How do we decide? First, we need to examine the influence we would trade by moving. I'm convinced part of Satan's plan is to lessen the impact of Christians through transience. The identity of the people of Jesus is to reflect the light of Christ. Think about the picture of a bunch of little lights exiting our cities in search of bigger spaces to shine. It's as if we're wanting our Maglite to get upgraded to stadium lighting somewhere else. Be careful of this subtle lie: "If the story of this city is greater maybe my life can have a bigger story too!"

We are all wired to make a huge splash in this world. That impulse is not wrong. But we need to be careful we aren't dreaming up a grand story for our lives to make us feel more significant. Maybe your story of accidentally ending up in your town isn't accidental after all. Maybe those who ended up back in their hometown aren't deadbeats. Maybe your view of success and upward mobility has been shaped more by the American Dream than the gospel. Maybe the grass isn't greener in the next urban pasture. Maybe the illusion you saw of "that other city" in a magazine is like an airbrushed model with no blemishes.

Stephanie had moved nineteen times in thirteen years, and she was tired of shifting sand beneath her feet. She didn't know it, but she was dying to grow roots. As she tried to straddle worlds between leadership in a church plant and a ragtag group of artists, she felt stuck. Stephanie began to resonate with the idea of staying put. She began to internalize the challenge to "live as if you're staying" and to love her city. She also began to understand the importance of art and culture in a city. Her city, like many that are revitalizing, desperately needs local artists to stay and help creativity take a deeper hold. Artists have the ability to create culture that can help others understand their place and even decide to grow roots there.

Today Stephanie is challenging other local artists to make the commitment to stay well. She doesn't have a formal leadership role, and she hasn't started a nonprofit, but she is an advocate, a herald for the message that she embodies as she takes the hard step of both committing to dwell well and "make a scene for Jesus." Stephanie wrote a poem to encapsulate her journey.

"LOVE YOUR CITY"

God I beg you, let me go.
Open any door!
Or open up a window,
Crack it ever so small and I'll fit through,
squeeze through,
ache through.
Let me go anywhere.
but here.
I want to go where things are
already happening cuz there isn't enough of me to
do good for the masses
here.
And if I can go there,
go to another place where the
cog is already making noise,
where the mission field is ripe
for the picking up,
then I won't have to
dig in
grow roots
plant deep.
That's where God found me!
Shipwrecked, beached like a whale
on the black sand of insecurity and addiction,
rescued I became.
Identity found as a kingdom keeper
and a maker.
Still weak and spread thin,
yet my tide was turning in
and the weight of the world was lifted
no longer was I the savior,
on the lookout to be the
change I wished I could be,
nor was I empty.
I drew breath from the never-ending source of

all of life ever lived!
My empathy and sympathy synced with the Creator of my
heartbeat so deep that it hurts most times.
And now my prayer is simple:
God, let me stay.
Close every door, lock every window.
Let me stay, let me live planted,
let me be one who can build relationships
that effect your kingdom come.
Let me love, as a reflection of your love for me.
Let me shine with the creativity
you knit deep within
my heart
and let it burst into this city.
Build your kindgom here,
and let me stay.
As a visionary, a mover, a shaker
a missionary
for it is my very great honor to
love your city like
you
did not come to be served
but to serve.

I see redemption all over Stephanie's journey. Many artists and makers are desperately trying to belong somewhere—and make a living on the side. We need more Stephanies in our cities who make the hard decision to gift their creativity to those around them instead of finding a destination city where these things are already in full swing. We need followers of Jesus in urban, suburban, rural, and university areas all over. Creatives reach other creatives, but they also wield tools to tell redemptive stories. We need to both challenge and make space for the creatives to know they and their work are welcome. Creatives can help the church "make a scene for Jesus" in unique ways in our places.

WHEN IS IT TIME TO GO?

Every time I talk about putting down roots, someone brings up the magic question: "When is it time to go?" This is a great question, but hard to answer. Here are a few principles that are crucial in determining when it's time to go.

When God tells you. Knowing when God has asked you to go is a bit like knowing when God has asked you to give. You might pass a panhandler ten times, but on the eleventh time you know you are supposed to empty your wallet. When God says, "Go," it's time to go. I know several people who have been told to go to a place they knew very little about—like Turkey, Pakistan, Colombia, or Des Moines. I also know many people who landed in my city because God told them to go. I met one couple in a coffee shop who were living out of their car. God told them to pack up their lives and move here. Now he is on staff at our church. "Go to a place I will show you" can be one of the biggest steps of faith you can take. Once you get there, just make sure to live like you're staying.

When going is really returning. Some of the healthiest churches I know started as homecomings. Often people are drawn away from home for a season, and something pulls them back. I have had many leaders describe a "man of Macedonia" moment to me where they realized the friends they grew up with were still lost and needed someone to introduce them to the way of Jesus. A church planter we've trained through Frontline Church Planting felt the call to leave Colorado and move back to his wife's hometown of Kenosha, Wisconsin. You know God is calling on the other end of the line when you leave Colorado for Wisconsin! Just sayin'. They have been received really well; they came in with credibility, stories, and family that most church planters don't have. They are finding themselves again in the context of a place they were already connected to.

When God crafts an opportunity specifically for you. Many friends describe moving to a place because "God wrote my job description." Some walked the ground and just knew they should invest in the people there. I often hear, "It just . . . fit!" Sometimes God shapes opportunities that fit us better than we could have ever known to dream for ourselves. Be careful not to use the God card, however, to indulge a move up in the world, into a bigger house, or into a job where you will feel more valued.

When God's provision is clear. I have watched several friends who were on the edge of poverty get blown away by God providing them an opportunity across the city or across the country. They moved so they could take care of pressing needs. They weren't looking to get rich, only to find a way to make it. Financial needs are real, and the bigger families get, the more we must pay attention to this reality.

When you have no choice. The military and some companies can transfer you wherever they want as long as you are committed to them. In that case you are changing locations, but you are staying inside a subculture where you have a unique influence. You can go to another physical place but "stay well" inside that organization.

When you are attending to a higher priority. After attending to a show by one of my favorite musicians, I got some time to chat with him. We talked about where home was for him when he was off the road. He and his wife were considering moving to Colorado, and of course, I affirmed this would be the right decision. I was surprised about where he lived, a small Southern town completely off the national grid of art and culture. He explained that his mother-in-law had lost her husband, and they had committed to move there for two years to grieve together. Sometimes staying well in close relationships needs to take a higher priority than staying in a place.

When God lights you up for a place. If you continue to pray about a place and you just can't get it out of your head, maybe God put that desire there. For about two years I felt selfish about living in Colorado. *Everyone wants to move to Colorado*, I thought. *It's beautiful and like a jungle gym for grown-ups.* Somewhere down deep I thought God really wanted to take me to a boring and lifeless place. In my last semester of college in the Midwest, I was offered a good job at a good church that was a good fit for me. The church was healthy, and the benefits were good. I was fifty-fifty, though. I talked it through with the lead pastor, and eventually he said, "Alan, you need to go to Colorado, don't you?" He saw it, and he called it out. He knew God had lit me up for Colorado. Now I know why.

QUESTIONS TO ASK BEFORE RELOCATING

Every opportunity to leave is a matter for discernment. There's no gondola ride up the mountain of relocation. It can feel more like hiking on a greased Slip'N Slide. It is not wrong to leave, but it's easy to leave for the wrong reasons. Maybe you are wanting more influence than you currently have, but maybe you are on the verge of reaching critical influence in the place you live. We must be on our knees to hear from the Father when opportunities present themselves. Our cities are gardens ready to be cultivated so the gospel can bear much fruit. Transplanting is a delicate business, and plants don't always take root again. I know people who have left and flourished, but I also know people who found the grass was not greener on the other side. Whatever decision you make isn't going to screw up God's plan, however. God is at work in your place. He's also at work in the place you are thinking of relocating to.

Here are some questions to guide you as you consider relocating.

- What unique influence would I forfeit by moving?
- What unique influence might God give me in the new place?
- Is my motivation driven by my desires or God's?

- How long could I see myself living in this new place?
- What is God already doing in this other place?
- What church family would be a good fit in this new place?
- Whom can I talk to who truly knows the cracks and beauty of this new community?
- What is the narrative of this new place, and am I ready to embrace that?

God's Kingdom reign is everywhere, but your placement is specific. It is dangerous to think God's reign is specific *and* we're supposed to have an impact everywhere. The body of Christ is universal, and sometimes we just don't trust God is at work in other neighborhoods, spheres of society, and cities without us. We don't bring God's work with us; we join it in the new place we go to. Church planters can often make the mistake of thinking, *Let's bring God to Minneapolis, Fort Collins, or Salem.* Last I checked, he's already there.

The fully human Jesus was limited to one place at one time. He would often scurry to other places when it was time to go, but he also stayed longer in some places than I would have imagined. And he stopped for longer periods than I would expect. As I read through the Gospels I often think, *You've only got three years to get through this region and accomplish a lot of work. Why are you taking a break?* Not only does Jesus' pattern demonstrate trust in the Father; it shows the significance of place. The next mission field is always calling, but we have to trust God and stay put if God has called us to impact people there. The fact that God would limit his son, Jesus, to taking on one place at a time should tell us something about limiting ourselves to a place.

When you have an entrepreneurial, naturally caffeinated, often-scattered wiring like I do, the staying message can be a tough pill to swallow. Being fully present where I am means pushing ten other ideas and places aside. The staying message is one I wrestle with every day. I want to seize every opportunity for Jesus, attend every gathering of believers, and connect with what God is doing all over. But I can't.

There's a pressure, even in ministry, to keep up with the Joneses. Sometimes this looks like hopping from place to place, speaking to different groups of people and challenging them with different things. But home is the great level playing field. There are always real challenges at home with friends, family, opponents, and people who drain you. There is also the always-challenging battle with overcommitment. The irony of national conferences is speakers in a building where their church does not gather, speaking to people they do not shepherd, on topics that were not birthed in that context. These gatherings are certainly valuable, but they aren't the end. Hopefully they're a means to challenge the body of Christ to greater impact in their particular place.

Some people are, indeed, called to national and even global influence, but that list is very small. They have sacrificed much to obey God and walk in this calling. This is also true of global or translocal missions. I know many people

who spend stints as missionaries and catalysts in other countries. They work really hard, and I am thankful they have
followed this call. But their path simply won't be the path
for most of us.

My main role as a pastor and equipper at our church is
to help people recognize how they can listen to God and
show him to others. People have huge fears about being on
mission in their neighborhood or workplace. There are a lot
of excuses why this is the hardest place to reach people and
why this is the hardest time to start doing it. The lawn will
never look good enough to host that barbecue; the time will
never seem perfect to share with that friend about Jesus; the
house will never look nice enough to host that dinner party.
Some of the best ministry happens when we invite people to
join us when it's inconvenient. When friends and neighbors
need to stop by most, the house might be a wreck and you
won't feel ready. A friend of mine constantly reminds me to
"embrace the interruptions."

Naturally, when people come over we want to give them
our best food, our cleanest home, and our most focused attention. It can be hard for me to welcome people in when my
house is a mess. As a dad of four kids, that mess happens in
about five minutes. Despite good intentions to make others
feel loved and cared for, I get sucked into promoting the
image of a calm and collected life. What I've found is people
often feel more loved and valued when my wife and I welcome them in during the mess of life. If we can't invite people
into our living room or dirty kitchen, we won't invite them

into the messy cracks in our lives. When we invite people into our messes, we are affirming they are welcome just as they are. People are more important than the prep we can make for them, and that should change everything.

So if you are thinking about staying, I challenge you to make a commitment to stay: grab a shovel and serve, dig into the soil in your place. Maybe you need to re-examine your motives for wanting to leave and ask the hard questions. Perhaps you are even at the edge of putting your house on the market for an upgrade, and you should choose to grow roots in your neighborhood. Work through the hard realities of what it would take to dwell well as a salty and illuminated champion of God's coming Kingdom.

QUESTIONS FOR REFLECTION AND DISCUSSION

What limitations frustrate you about your place or your existing relationships?

Is your home a fortress from life or a hub for life? What fears do you need to let go of to take on more of a ministry hub mentality?

What fears are standing in the way of your making a solid commitment to your place?

9

STAY FORTH!

"Pilgrims are poets who create by taking journeys."
RICHARD NIEBUHR

"Above all trust in the slow work of God. We are quite naturally impatient in everything to reach the end without delay."
PIERRE TEILHARD DE CHARDIN

"Love your neighbors—not the neighbors you pick out but the ones you have."
WENDELL BERRY

OUR CULTURE SUBTLY praises those who move up by moving out and moving on. From the Manifest Destiny of the mid-nineteenth century to the Go Forth ad campaign from Levi's in the early twenty-first century, the spirit of America is based on exploration and expansion. It represents adventure, exploration, and conquest. It represents, oddly enough, the status quo. We praise those who *go* to college away from home, those who *go* visit places as tourists and missionaries, those who *go* change the world beyond the place of their birth. Going is exciting and pregnant with possibility.

149

The urge to go forth can accidentally lift our eyes past the local.

I believe the paradigm needs to shift from Go Forth to Stay Forth. People everywhere are discovering how the posture of staying forth—applying that same spirit of exploration to the place we find ourselves—can be exhilarating. What if we channeled all our enthusiasm for travel, exploration, and service back into our cities? There is adventure right under our noses. There are people who need to know Jesus in our neighborhoods, relationships we can deepen, local risks even greater than crossing continents.

Just to be clear, we don't want to kill the spirit of exploration—we need it! We need to channel and refocus the God-given urges among us. This chapter will explore practical ways to live the adventure and challenge of staying forth.

DO SMALL THINGS

"You're going to do *big* things for God!" I remember the time someone told me this in college. I wondered if I needed to start an organization for AIDS victims, move to South America, or become a megachurch pastor. *What if God only wants me to accomplish something small?* I wondered. *Would I be a failure? What if I moved to a relatively normal place and was faithful right there?* My head was spinning needlessly in a million different directions.

Some phrases Christians toss around rub me the wrong way. With the best intentions, we often underplay the small things. Many Christian leaders suffer from "ministry shame" born out of unrealistic expectations.[1] After dreaming massive dreams and embracing massive visions for what we can change, we meet reality. Paul Hiebert sees unrealistic expectations as dangerous: "We feel guilty because we cannot live up to our own expectations. We are angry because no one told us it would be this way, and because we make such slow progress in adjusting to the new culture."[2]

That probably doesn't sound encouraging to you. Here's the good news: If you stay in a place and keep making an effort to understand the people, rhythms, and culture there, you will eventually get over the hump. You will eventually understand and be understood. You will eventually have influence. You will eventually get a grip on realistic expectations.

If you're in it for the long haul, eventually you will hit a moment when you ask, "Is *this* it? Is this all?" One of the most common themes of the missional roundtables we host is the challenge of learning the long-term realities of a place, and coming back to earth from a sky-high vision. You have to push through these challenges to find the resolve to stay. Maybe you've thought, *This isn't what the books hyped up*, or *Why didn't my story turn out like theirs?* Don't judge your hardest days by someone else's epic days.

This watershed moment is when it becomes crucial to create support systems for yourself. You need the support of people in the same trenches you're in, not just the financial and prayer support of your mailing list. Part of the practicality of staying is finding people who "get you" and can appreciate what you're going through. Knowing and being known by others is a basic human need. Far too often people trying to make a difference in the name of Jesus begin to live by the following: "We are part of a missionary community made up of strong-willed strangers to whom we do not dare admit our weakness, and there may be no one to pastor us when we fail."[3] We must learn instead to develop communities of caring companions, invested advocates who form an ecosystem of Kingdom work around us. These fellow missionaries and committed "stayers" will help sustain you on the good and bad days on the bipolar journey of a life on mission with God. They will remind you the Holy Spirit is still with you and God is still on his throne. They will remind you they love you, and you are going to be okay.

TAKE COMFORT; THE BAR IS LOW

I will never forget my first morning in our apartment after getting married. My wife and I had returned from an amazing honeymoon in the Caribbean. Still a little crispy with sunburn, we were ready to live happily ever after. I woke up, eager to show Julie that sharing a place with me would be a great honor for her, so I began to make the bed.

Suddenly I stopped. *I can't do this. Then she'll expect it every day for the rest of my life!* So I left the bed unmade and went to the kitchen to make breakfast.

What can I say? I aim to impress. I was very conscious to set the bar low.

We can take comfort that the bar for community in North America is really low. This is actually good news! Any attempt at faithful presence, no matter how small, will be noticed. This is perfect grounds for experimentation in our neighborhoods, at our workplaces, and among our friends. Faithful presence is not about scoring touchdowns but about pushing the ball down the field. The relational gains might feel slow, but when pursued faithfully, they are steady. Build off small wins like a breakthrough conversation, an opportunity to help a neighbor lift something, attending a friend's birthday, or a tool you can let someone borrow. Almost any effort you make to be neighborly and loving is a step up from what people expect.

GROW SOME ROOTS!

You will need to make specific and intentional shifts in order to become more rooted in the lives and rhythms of the places, spaces, and people around you. Get practical and get on your knees before God. Here are a few places you can get started.

Be intentional in your job. There is a lot of potential to influence those you work with. Ben Connelly and Bob Roberts suggest that "even if you have the opportunity for a corner office, choose a space you can interact with coworkers." They also suggest that you "invite coworkers into non-work life: After a few meals or drinks invite them to your home, family and community. Make individual relationships corporate through meals and hobbies."[4] You can set aside one day a week as coworker lunch day. Challenge yourself to invite a new person or group out to lunch every week.

Make a "roots commitment" to your place. One risk you

can take is to join with others to commit five, ten, or fifteen years to your place. Share your commitment with those close to you, and come up with a few aims you have for dwelling well. This can be one of the most powerful covenants you and your family make.

Plan something public. I recommend starting with a block party, a deck party, or BBQ on a warm night. Who doesn't love a party and grilling out? Make sure to have black bean or quinoa burgers available for those averse to consuming animals. It's an easy way to get most of your neighbors in the same place at the same time. Cookie exchanges during the holidays, a driveway party on Halloween, or a community yard sale are other good ways to start. Having this in your front yard or street allows for unintimidating social space. If you don't find a way to meet and gather with neighbors, it will be hard to actually love them.

Listen and dream. Listen intently to the needs and desires of neighbors and friends. Read community forums, analyze the needs in the neighborhood, talk to community officials, and do something meaningful and consistent to fill one crack around you. Talk to others about this and create a team. Don't go it alone, and don't try to fill all the needs you uncover! You will need to submit to others' ideas, because their dreams won't always match yours. Some of the most impactful serving opportunities our missional community has engaged in were things I was not personally passionate about, and at the beginning I didn't see the value in them.

Try crazy and simple ideas. Over the past years of serving collectively as a group, I have come to realize that some of our craziest ideas have catalyzed mission in incredible ways. The most effective ideas sounded either too simple or too crazy to actually work. We have seen simple and crazy ideas lead to incredible avenues of embodying the life of Jesus.

THE BASEMENT CONCERT SERIES

One of our crazy ideas rose from the realization that there were very few places for musicians to get discovered in our city. During one season I watched many great musicians move away to more music-friendly cities to make great culture there. This grieved me. How would our arts culture ever grow, and how would artists and culture makers ever make a scene for Jesus in our city?

My wife has wisely learned to be a little skeptical of my crazy ideas, but we decided to launch the Basement Concert Series that winter. We set up our big, boxy basement as a concert venue, and nine different acts filled up our basement for three different shows. Bands would play for free, and those in attendance would put $5 in the pot toward the ministry, charity, or struggling family we had decided in advance to bless. Friends showed up who wouldn't come to a Bible study or church gathering. We packed people in pretty tight and served way too much coffee. The next winter we had visual artists donate pieces to be sold for more profit to go to the chosen cause.

Basement concerts are beautifully chaotic. Friends, neighbors, and strangers cram into our basement and stay to eat dessert around our dinner table. A young woman who is part of our missional community, Kimberly, invited friends from her college class to one of our concerts, which happened to take place over their spring break. One of her friends seemed to be having a decent time. But then one of the musicians shared about how Jesus was healing her marriage. I wondered if this unexpected testimony would make Kimberly's friend feel like she had been the recipient of the classic bait 'n' switch. But when Kimberly returned to school on Monday, the teacher asked the class, "What was the highlight of your spring break?" Kimberly's friend raised her hand and said, "I went to the coolest concert ever! The people were so welcoming, the music was great, and I left with care packages to give away to the homeless." Suddenly the whole class was interested in crashing our next crazy idea.

DARE TO DREAM

The older we get, the sillier dreaming can feel. However insignificant they feel, dreams are not a waste of your time and energy. Keep exercising your incarnational imagination. Dreams are crucial for working toward the good of a place. I have formed a list of dreams and ideas for the community around us:

- Host a formal outdoor banquet for my neighbors.
- Get to know our new mailman as well as we knew our last mailman.

- Throw a party for all the teachers and administration from the local elementary school.

- Host a nationally known band in our local park free of charge.

- Become the first person the school office calls when a crisis hits.

- Create a phone tree for neighborhood birthdays.

- Throw a block party at least once a year.

- Partner to purchase a rental home for church planters entering our city that can become a hub for faithful neighborhood presence.

- Become a religious advisor to a local political leader.

- Become a listening ear for my kids' school principal.

- Host a driveway party every other Halloween.

- Repurpose an eyesore building in my city into a concert and wedding venue.

- Create a fund for friends who are adopting.

- Partner to start a church-based employment network for ex-felons.

- Become my kids' favorite sports coach.

- See a web of leaders arise in our city who help challenge others to stay.

- Help churches partner to take bigger risks together than they would take apart.

These ideas might seem ridiculous, but I am still dreaming about how God could use them. I have no idea if these will come to pass, but I am determined to never stop dreaming about how God can work through crazy ideas.

IDEAS FOR STAYING FORTH

By far the most effective thing in helping people gain a Kingdom foothold in their neighborhood has been stories. Stories both validate and encapsulate how we join God in the renewal of all things. Most people are not innovators, although we all like to think we are. If we are going to inspire people to stay forth, we need to tell stories of ordinary heroes living in the way of Jesus.

Create a host space. A church community remodeled their building around the idea of serving and hosting their local community. They cannot actually fit their whole church in their community space—at least that's what the fire marshal would say. But by being intentional they have hosted countless groups that engage and champion their community. Community organizations and nonprofits have used their building for events and office space.

Gather around what your community celebrates. A new church launched in an urban pocket full of art and expression in a town with a reputation for sorcery. My friend began to engage art as a means to connect with people. After building a relationship with many in the arts community, he decided to launch an art and faith discussion group at the local gallery. This gallery and café has become a median space for him, and he is being intentional to stay well there.

They have seen a lot of traction through the art groups, and even had a season where they featured classic religious art pieces for discussion. Each year the church hosts the Redemptive Art Show, where they invite artists who are Jesus-followers and some who aren't to show and explain pieces with a redemptive theme. Christian artists are able to share their story and the truth of how the Great Artist inspires their art. This town celebrates art and is well aware there is a church in town that celebrates it as well.

Get into the sports community. Two of my friends came to town looking for their missional niche in a nicer part of our city. They knew they wouldn't be doing homeless ministry like their friends downtown. Instead, they made the local YMCA their hub as coaches and active members. They became known there and invested in many people in that community. People have come to know Jesus through their influence there, and they continue to coach teams whenever they can.

Fill a community need. After less than a year in their community, a church in the Northeast realized their town lacked a farmers' market. Although none of their core team produced veggies and fruit for this, they became relational brokers and worked toward launching a farmers' market every Saturday in the summer. Now the community gathers because a church dared to fill a community need.

Join other rhythms. Football has become a connecting

point for a lot of people I know. A big game is an easy invite. A lot of folks I know create a rhythm of either hosting for every game or going over to a friend's house for every game. You will have hours between plays to catch up on life.

Build off small connections. There are several apple trees in our neighborhood. This past summer I started to notice the apples growing sooner and bigger than previous years. I set the goal of making homegrown, homemade apple cider. The neighbor behind me and the one across the street had apple trees also, so I decided to make the ask. They were thrilled to let me pick some apples for the batch. The men helped my family pick them and took great joy in seeing us put them to use. I had struggled to connect with those two men previously. Trips back to their house for their share of the cider made conversation much easier. The cider season has been the breakthrough I needed to make deeper connection with them.

Create regular relational traditions. Free Coffee Friday has been a huge win to connect with neighbors and school parents. This tradition has led to birthday parties, prayer for people in hard situations, and long conversations about the beauty and depravity of life. Some folks have weekly traditions of lawn games, cookouts, and kids' playtimes at the same park during the summer. Some folks organize the annual neighborhood garage sale or make the same baked goods for neighbors each year.

Cultivate front yard community. Growing up in suburbia, my wife and I were used to playing and partying in the backyard. Our relationships grew as we shifted our fun to the front. We moved our grill, kept our lawn chairs handy, and set up a small café table next to the driveway, where we can watch the kids ride bikes and have easy access to conversations.

Party with neighbors, not just friends. We put our focus on partying with our neighbors instead of our existing friends. We used to invite our friends from all over to Christmas parties and cookouts at our house; now we invite our neighbors first and our existing friends when appropriate. It's through parties and gatherings that our neighbors have become our friends.

Live intentionally and avoid extra stuff. Most people don't have much extra capacity, but they can shift things they are already doing to have more intention. I encourage you to wrestle through how what you are *already* doing can be expanded to include neighbors and friends who are far from Jesus. Almost anything you do can be an opportunity to bring others into your routine. Focus on things that are a priority for you—working out at the gym, playing basketball, going to yard sales—and invite others to join you.

Neighbor nights. Some friends of ours pondered how they could challenge their small group to love their neighbors well. Every family in their group committed to hosting a "neighbor night" on the same evening. They created different spaces to connect with their neighbors based on their own personalities. Some threw a block party, others invited their neighbors for dessert, and still others hosted a game night.

One of the couples built on the relationships that began on neighbor night; they have maintained a steady focus and reliable presence in their neighborhood.

One night these friends got an emergency call from a neighbor. She was about to deliver her baby, and she knew that this woman worked at a hospital. She ran to this woman's home and calmed her down until an ambulance arrived. The woman was rushed to the hospital and delivered shortly after arriving. Our friend nearly delivered a baby in her neighborhood! Now that's the adventure of faithful presence!

A NEW WAY TO COUNT

The deeper I delve into the guts of incarnational living, the more questions people ask. By this point you've likely been asking the magic question, "What *counts* as mission?" It feels strange asking this, but it's actually a crucial question. We need to rethink and unlearn a lot.

In their book *The New Parish*, the founders of the Parish Collective say that learning to see all the forces at play in a neighborhood

> will require a new lens. It will require a new
> imagination that expands beyond our current
> concept of church and begins to track new patterns
> of renewal at work in the world. Ultimately, learning
> to see will require reorientation, new postures and
> new ways of practicing faith.[5]

In addition to new lenses, imagination, orientation, and practices, we must develop new metrics. North Americans are calculated and driven people. Our businesses and non-profits focus highly on living out mission and creating certain results. We have to understand what "counts" when living out incarnational mission and faithful presence, or we will be chasing the wind. If staying forth is the new future, we will have to leave some old measurements behind. Here are a few benchmarks that can start to form your new journey into staying. Get creative and add some metrics of your own.

Dirty carpet. The other day I found myself getting frustrated at how often we have to get our carpets steam cleaned. Then I realized, *This is a great problem to have!* My kids aren't to blame for our stained carpets; they're stained from regularly opening our home to a lot of people.

Counting question: How many people enter your house in the course of a month? How many of those people don't know Jesus? How many of those people experienced God's Kingdom and a community of people in your home?

Lingering. We all know the feeling of people lingering too long in our home. Sometimes this is too much, and it's time to get direct about people heading out. But I have learned to appreciate the lingering process. Kids play in the front yard as we talk to parents; we wash dishes as people sit at our table; that person who is struggling hangs around to chat a little longer.

Learn to linger well! People often linger because they want to ask deeper questions than the social environment would allow. Good conversations happen, and lingering is a sign others are comfortable enough to stay when everyone else has gone.

Counting question: How many people have lingered in your home this month?

Last-minute favors. American life embodies two things in regards to community: private and planned. We have to plan our lives and time with people, or they will plan us. But there's another side to this coin: we know we are getting close to others when they stop in on us unplanned, or they call us in the moment needing help. My wife and I get a lot of opportunities to help parents through spur-of-the-moment requests to bring their kids home from school, help with a quick moving project, lend a lawnmower, or bring over some sugar. You know people are getting comfortable with you when they start to inconvenience you.

Counting question: How many last-minute favors have friends and neighbors asked of you this month?

Meals. Perhaps the best investment of time and money we can make is in eating meals together. Jesus invested a lot of his time here. People always connect over food, so lunches and dinner parties can be a great launching pad for gaining relational equity.

Counting question: How many meals have you shared with people far from the church this month?

Seized opportunities. We need to be ready to grab fruitful opportunities that present themselves. Off-the-cuff conversations, unexpected vulnerability, even surprising health issues and tragic events can lead us to unpredictable and off-the-grid gospel opportunities that can bear much fruit.

Counting question: How many unexpected opportunities have you seized for the sake of embodying and proclaiming the gospel?

Intentionally missed opportunities. True love is tested by our affections for other people or things. In a world of upward mobility, you will likely be offered jobs elsewhere and given the opportunity to relocate. It's easy to accept these without thought, because it's natural to believe promotion is the natural way to success. What if we viewed these decisions through an incarnational lens? We would consider how many relationships we would need to step out of, and how much relational equity we would be forfeiting.

Counting question: How many times have you denied a "better" opportunity elsewhere because you have meaningful roots?

Invitations to community boards. Chalk it up as a success when you get invited onto a board in your community, at the local school, or in the chamber of commerce. This means you are viewed not just as one *of* your community but one *for* your community. Someone sees you as an advocate! Yes, you are busy and have priorities, but you should always try to say yes to these opportunities.

Counting question: How many invitations have you had to serve on a community board or leadership team? How many of these invitations have you accepted?

Celebrations. Every human desires to be celebrated. Birthdays, wedding anniversaries, sobriety anniversaries, out-of-debt parties, retirement parties, garden harvest celebrations, and adoption "gotcha days" are only the tip of the iceberg. We need to be masters of creating reasons to make a big deal about people. I'll never forget celebrating our longtime mailman Jake's retirement. Jake stayed well, served faithfully, and was more than just a postal worker. He cared deeply about people, and people cared deeply about him. Neighbors started a campaign collecting money to buy Jake and his wife gift cards. Our family threw a block party to honor him. We had a ceremony to share why Jake is the best mailman in the world. Jake shed a few tears that night.

Counting question: How have you creatively celebrated those around you?

AN ART, NOT A SCIENCE

In *The Art of Neighboring* Dave Runyon and Jay Pathak write about their journey from busy neighbors to neighboring catalysts. They ask the dangerous question, "What if Jesus actually wanted us to love our physical neighbors?" As the title of their book says, intentional gospel presence is an art, not a science. I'd love to create a roadmap or instruction manual, but it wouldn't help much. My hope is that in this book you've been given a few key principles, permission to dream, new metrics, and encouraging stories of those taking the risk to grow roots.

God is patient. He doesn't expect you to embrace a Stay Forth vision today, tomorrow, or this year. In fact, staying well isn't a destination; it's a journey of slowly extending roots into the soil so you have more capacity to grow fruit.

Try something. Take two big risks this year. Sign a covenant to be faithfully present in your city. If you're not clear why you're trying to move across town, consider taking your house off the market. Fall in love with longevity. Pray for those who are closest to you. Love the least of these and the greatest of these in your community. Live out of a gospel willfulness, not just an emotionally appealing gospel. Mark Labberton calls this the "dangerous act of loving your neighbor."[6] I dare you to enter this beautifully dangerous space.

Your city is different than mine. Your neighborhood is different than mine. Your relationships are different than mine. Instead of getting a seven-step plan to dwell well, you will need to pick up your brushes and learn fresh techniques to paint the canvas God is already working on in your place. There are beautiful paintings that God is working on all over. They look as different from each other as Picassos and Warhols. They are all beautiful.

Perhaps you are wondering why you read this whole book. You haven't heard anything impressive or explosive. This book has been less about tactics and more about a way of life, postures, and rhythms. Strategies wear out with time, but proper rhythms mature us and give us ever-expanding influence.

We discover something in moments of quiet faithfulness that we can't learn in the university, the stadium, or the webinar. Just because the ordinary things don't equate to much in this world doesn't mean they don't matter to God and to others. Finding the value of quiet faithfulness, of faithful presence, will require you to swap out the lenses from the kingdom of this world to the Kingdom of God. You might not get attaboys, but you will find the joy of partnering with the triune God in the most countercultural ways.

In case you're wondering, God is already at work in your friends, your neighbors, and your city. You don't need to take him anywhere. The battle for people is not your battle; it's his. It's not your ministry; it's his. We are returning to things, people, and places that we have drifted away from. This will bring us to our knees in dependence upon our God as it brings us into relationship with those around us. Our eyes have been veiled for too long, pointed too high on the horizon.

May your eyes shift from where you could be to where you already are.
May global adventures become local as distant humans become near souls.
May you serve and befriend, and have others do the same to you.
May staying with God's hand excite you as much as finding your destiny.
May your enamored heart find focus.
May your life be described as salty and luminous.
May you be as content on two wheels and on two feet as you are between
two wings.
May you dwell well even when you haven't planned well.
May you have the courage to see the mission field right in front of your face.
May you be known for nearness and here-ness to those around you.
May the Keeper keep you engaged and reengaged in his Kingdom work.

I lift up my eyes to the hills.
From where does my help come?
My help comes from the LORD,
who made heaven and earth.
He will not let your foot be moved;
he who keeps you will not slumber.
Behold, he who keeps Israel
will neither slumber nor sleep.
The LORD is your keeper;
the LORD is your shade on your right hand.
The sun shall not strike you by day,
nor the moon by night.
The LORD will keep you from all evil;
he will keep your life.
The LORD will keep
your going out and your coming in
from this time forth and forevermore.

PSALM 121

QUESTIONS FOR REFLECTION AND DISCUSSION

How is God uniquely painting on the canvas of your place?

What adjustments do you need to make to your ministry metrics?

What two risks can you take this year to connect deeper to those around you?

Acknowledgments

Vanguard Church leaders: Thanks for not compromising the mission. You have always given me the freedom to be me.

Kelly and Tosha Williams: Thanks for going, but thanks more for staying.

David Zimmerman: You have been a joy to work with. You know how words matter in shaping God's unfolding story.

Colorado Church Planters: You inspire me. I can't believe I get to work with you all. God knows all the sacrifices you've made to stay.

Don Pape: Thanks for believing in this message and having great taste in breakfast joints. Next one is on me.

Alan Hirsch and Michael Frost: Thanks for being missional before it was a word and for calling the American Church back to loving our place. Keep beating that drum, mates.

My brother, J. R.: You have gone before me in everything, and I'm grateful for that. You are courageous beyond belief.

Mom and Dad: You embodied a gospel we could taste, touch, and smell. Thanks for accidentally training two pastors.

Drew Dyck: You realized people needed to hear this message before I did.

Matt and Shaina: Thanks for taking a risk on us. Without your risk we could not have taken ours.

Clay and Bill: You have dreamed contagious dreams for our place.

Yemi: You embody the heart of this book. So glad you and Abbey have made this city your nest.

Everyone mentioned in this book: The faithfulness of your life has shaped me in one way or another. Press on!

Notes

INTRODUCTION

1. Eugene H. Peterson, *The Pastor* (San Francisco: HarperOne, 2012), 218.

CHAPTER 1: THE RESURRECTION OF PLACE

1. Alvin Toffler, *Future Shock* (Toronto: Bantam Books, 1970), 75.
2. Paul Sparks, Tim Soerens, and Dwight J. Friesen, *The New Parish* (Downers Grove, IL: IVP Books, 2014), 181.
3. Eugene H. Peterson, *The Pastor* (San Francisco: HarperOne, 2012), 247.
4. Jamie Arpin-Ricci, personal correspondence with the author.
5. Peterson, *Pastor*, 216.
6. Paul G. Hiebert, *Anthropological Insights for Missionaries* (Grand Rapids, MI: Baker Academic, 1986), 61.
7. Hiebert, *Anthropological Insights for Missionaries*, 61.
8. Jonathan Wilson-Hartgrove, *The Wisdom of Stability* (Brewster, MA: Paraclete Press, 2010), 92.
9. Peterson, *Pastor*, 190.
10. See David R. Wheeler, "Higher Calling, Lower Wages: The Vanishing of the Middle-Class Clergy," *The Atlantic*, July 22, 2014, http://www.theatlantic.com/business/archive/2014/07/higher-calling-lower-wages-the-collapse-of-the-middle-class-clergy/374786/.
11. I got this idea from my friend Bryan Barley.
12. Michael Frost, *Incarnate: The Body of Christ in an Age of Disengagement* (Downers Grove, IL: IVP Books, 2014), p.155.

CHAPTER 2: BIKES, GARDENS, AND FORGOTTEN PLACES

1. The idea of finding where God is at work and joining him there was first introduced by Henry T. Blackaby and Claude V. King in the book *Experiencing God* (Nashville: Lifeway, 1990).
2. To learn more about Braddock, see TED talks by the mayor, John Fetterman, by searching for his name at http://tedxtalks.ted.com.
3. Joseph R. Myers, *The Search to Belong* (Grand Rapids, MI: Zondervan/ Youth Specialties, 2003), 120.
4. For a deeper look at the value of the table in community, I recommend Tim Chester, *A Meal with Jesus* (Wheaton, IL: Crossway, 2011), and Leonard Sweet, *From Tablet to Table* (Colorado Springs: NavPress, 2015).
5. Myers, *The Search to Belong*, 126.

CHAPTER 3: THE STORY BEHIND YOUR PLACE

1. Jon Huckins and Jon Hall, "Localism and Gentrification," in *Vespas, Cafés, Singlespeed Bikes, and Urban Hipsters,* ed. Sean Benesh (Portland, OR: Urban Loft, 2014), 282.
2. Paul Sparks, Tim Soerens, and Dwight J. Friesen, *The New Parish* (Downers Grove, IL: IVP Books, 2014), 148.

CHAPTER 4: A ROOTED GOSPEL

1. I always recommend missionaries and church planters read *The Celtic Way of Evangelism* to glean principles of gospel contextualization. George G. Hunter III, *The Celtic Way of Evangelism*, 10th anniversary ed. (Nashville: Abingdon Press, 2010).
2. I originally got the idea of "people texture" versus "people study" from my friend Geoff Surratt.
3. Paul Sparks, Tim Soerens, and Dwight J. Friesen, *The New Parish* (Downers Grove, IL: IVP Books, 2014), 23.
4. Jon Tyson, "The Secret to Sustaining Incarnational Mission," video, streaming at http://verge279.rssing.com/browser. php?indx=25823971&item=16.

CHAPTER 5: THE GLORY OF THE MUNDANE

1. Eugene H. Peterson, *The Pastor* (San Francisco: HarperOne, 2012), 208.

CHAPTER 6: THE RISK OF WINGS

1. Billy Bragg, "Something Happened," *Mr. Love and Justice* (Anti Records, 2008).
2. Peter Berger, *The Homeless Mind* (New York: Vintage, 1974), 77.

3. Michael Frost and Alan Hirsch, *The Faith of Leap* (Grand Rapids, MI: Baker Books, 2011), 182.

4. Frost and Hirsch, *Faith of Leap*, 183

5. Emily T. Wierenga, "Why I'm Not Always Opposed to Religious Tourism," October 10, 2014, http://www.thegospelcoalition.org/article/why-im-not-always-opposed-to-religious-tourism.

CHAPTER 7: THE RISK OF ROOTS

1. Jonathan Wilson-Hartgrove, *The Wisdom of Stability* (Brewster, MA: Paraclete Press, 2010), 140.

2. Paul G. Hiebert, *Anthropological Insights for Missionaries* (Grand Rapids, MI: Baker Academic, 1986), 65.

3. Rodney Stark, *The Rise of Christianity* (San Francisco: HarperOne, 1997), 83.

4. Stark, *Rise of Christianity*, 83.

5. Stark, *Rise of Christianity*, 93.

6. Stark, *Rise of Christianity*, 82-83.

7. Ann Coulter, "Ebola Doc's Condition Downgraded to 'Idiotic,'" August 6, 2014, http://www.anncoulter.com/columns/2014-08-06.html.

8. Tim Swarens, "Ebola Survivor Dr. Kent Brantly Answered Call to Serve," *Indianapolis Star*, November 6, 2014, http://www.indystar.com/story/opinion/columnists/tim-swarens/2014/11/06/swarens-ebola-survivor-dr-kent-brantly-answered-call-serve/18619087.

9. Swarens, "Ebola Survivor Dr. Kent Brantly Answered Call to Serve."

10. Leonard Hjalmarson, *Introduction to a Theology of Place* (Seattle, WA: CreateSpace, 2014), 55.

11. Hiebert, *Anthropological Insights for Missionaries*, 75.

12. Hiebert, *Anthropological Insights for Missionaries*, 68.

13. Hiebert, *Anthropological Insights for Missionaries*, 74.

14. Hjalmarson, *Introduction to a Theology of Place*, 21.

CHAPTER 8: SALT, LIGHT, AND SHOVELS

1. Michael J. McManus, "Christians Want Pittsburgh Known for God as Well as Steel," *Lakeland Ledger*, May 7, 1983.

2. Michael J. Sider-Rose, *Taking the Gospel to the Point* (Pittsburgh, PA: Pittsburgh Leadership Foundation, 2000), is the best place to get the complete picture of the story of God's work during that time.

3. Sider-Rose, *Taking the Gospel to the Point*, 37.

4. Jamie Arpin-Ricci, e-mail correspondence.

5. Rodney Stark, *The Rise of Christianity* (San Francisco: HarperOne, 1997), p. 3.
6. Stark, *The Rise of Christianity*, 208.
7. Sean Benesh, ed., *Vespas, Cafés, Singlespeed Bikes, and Urban Hipsters* (Portland, OR: Urban Loft, 2014), 247.
8. Michael Frost, *Surprise the World* (Colorado Springs: NavPress, 2016).
9. Dave Runyon, e-mail correspondence.
10. Jamie Arpin-Ricci, e-mail correspondence.

CHAPTER 9: STAY FORTH
1. I highly recommend the book *Fail* (Downers Grove, IL: InterVarsity Press, 2014) by my brother, J. R. Briggs. This book addresses the topic of shame largely born out of unrealistic expectations.
2. Paul G. Hiebert, *Anthropological Insights for Missionaries* (Grand Rapids, MI: Baker Academic, 1986), 70.
3. Hiebert, *Anthropological Insights for Missionaries*, 73.
4. Ben Connelly and Bob Roberts Jr., *A Field Guide for Everyday Mission* (Chicago: Moody Press, 2014), 55.
5. Paul Sparks, Tim Soerens, and Dwight J. Friesen, *The New Parish* (Downers Grove, IL: IVP Books, 2014), 30.
6. *The Dangerous Act of Loving Your Neighbor* (Downers Grove, IL: IVP Books, 2010) is the title of a book by Mark Labberton.

Frontline exists to equip the saints to multiply
DISCIPLES >> LEADERS >> CHURCHES.

Every church—big and small, new and old—can multiply, and we want to help.

Frontline connects and equips leaders in the following ways:

- Monthly on-the-ground equipping for everyday missionaries, church planters, and church leaders
- Frontline Church Planting residency
- Online training and coaching
- Church multiplication consulting
- Network gatherings, roundtables, and meetups
- Our annual MULTIPLY conference in Colorado

FrontlineChurchPlanting.com

FRONTLINE
CHURCH
PLANTING

DISCIPLES LEADERS CHURCHES

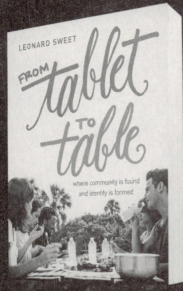

DO YOU EVER FEEL LIKE YOU'RE COMPLETELY MISSING THE POINT?

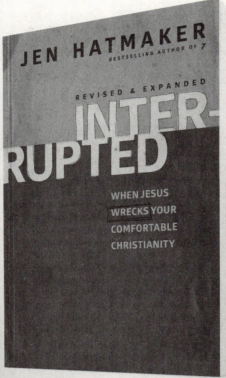

Interrupted | $14.99
978-1-63146-353-2

If you have felt restless in your faith, wondering if you are completely missing the point, then Jesus may be getting ready to Interrupt—right down to your lifestyle. That's certainly what happened to author Jen Hatmaker. What began with a prayer to "raise up in me a holy passion" ended with a faith journey to serve the last, the least, the forgotten, and the forsaken.

Find your copy wherever books are sold.